The Art of Witty Banter:
Be Clever, Quick, & Magnetic

By Patrick King
Social Interaction and
Conversation Coach at
www.PatrickKingConsulting.com

Table of Contents

Table of Contents 5

Chapter 1. Flow Like a River.....................7
Never Speak in Absolutes...................... 10
Think Before You React......................... 22
Practice Free Association..................... 31
Use Double Explanations 40
More Effective Compliments............... 47

Chapter 2. Conversation Is Play 65
Break the Fourth Wall........................... 66
The "Us Against the World" Technique
.... 72
Use Fallback Stories............................... 81
Instant Role Play 89

Chapter 3. A Touch of Witty Banter ... 103
The Witty Comeback Machine.......... 109
Instigate a Banter Chain 121
Go Beyond the Literal.......................... 132
The Art of Misconstruing................... 137

Chapter 4. Funny on Command 153
Vivid Imagery... 154
The Comic Triple................................... 166
Misdirection Aplenty 176

Chapter 5. Captivating Stories 203

A Life of Stories.. 205
The 1:1:1 Method 212
The Story Spine... 218
Inside Stories... 227
Ask for Stories.. 230

Summary Guide 245

Chapter 1. Flow Like a River

When I was growing up, my favorite television show wasn't one of the conventional cartoons like *G.I. Joe* or *X-Men*.

People tend to assume I had a sad childhood when I say this, but it's not that I was deprived of cartoons by draconian parents.

Cartoons typically aired early on weekend mornings, which meant you had to go to bed early the night before to get up in time for the shows. I always overslept, so I never saw the cartoons. But why was I oversleeping?

Because I always stayed up late to watch David Letterman, the host of *The Late Show with David Letterman* for over thirty years.

I didn't know it at the time, but of all the late-night television hosts, David Letterman was one of the most legendary. I just watched because I thought his Top Ten Lists were funny in an adult way that I couldn't quite understand. He would talk about economics, and though I didn't quite grasp the specifics, I knew the general feeling he was trying to convey and would laugh when my older brother laughed. I didn't get many of the digs and jabs he would take at guests, but I saw a specific tone and facial expression and went along with it.

It wasn't until I grew older that I started to really notice the subtle tactics Letterman used to energize boring guests and turn dull segments into funny ones.

In particular, it was his ability to banter wittily with his band leader, guests, and even himself in a self-deferential way that was the engine of the show. Letterman was like Teflon—he was so smooth and slick, he could always go with the flow, nothing ever seemed to faze him, and he was never without a witty quip or two.

It seemed as if he could joke about anything, and his jokes never seemed forced or out of place. It didn't work as well for me when I tried emulating Letterman the next day at school, but it did get me thinking about what constituted a person who was conversationally so slick and smooth, so able to let anything negative roll right off of them, that they were Teflon.

How can you not just always have something to say, but always have something witty and clever to say? Witty banter is many things at once—disarming, charming, intelligent, and quick. It almost sounds impossible when you think about the effects it has on others.

But banter is a skill just like pitching a baseball or underwater basket weaving. Once you know the patterns and building blocks, you can practice and improve them. And once you practice enough, they become instinct and habit that come easily to you because they are second nature.

This book is going to be one of your best tools for becoming adept at the kind of witty banter that will help you succeed in social situations.

You'll learn what makes a statement clever, how to deliver it quickly, and how it all comes together to make you someone of note and worth talking to. We'll start with techniques for flowing conversation. You can't achieve wit if you're caught in awkward silence!

Never Speak in Absolutes

Don't mind the irony in the section title (using the word "never" to warn against using the word "never"). But I stand by it.

One of the most common ways to kill any kind of conversational flow, regardless of how interesting the topic might be, is when one of the speakers reduces their questions to absolutes. Absolutes are tough to answer and sometimes even to contemplate, as you're about to read.

I was once set upon with absolute questions by a cousin at a family gathering. He was eight at the time, so it was excusable, but I'll never forget how it felt when someone kept talking to me in absolutes.

He asked me what my favorite ice cream flavor in the entire world was. I thought for a while and said rocky road. He started howling that I had horrible taste and demanding to know how I could forget Neapolitan. Next, he asked me what my favorite television show of all time was, and so on. It was a tortuous conversation full of long pauses and subsequent judgment of my tastes and opinions.

Years later, he would discover that he was lactose intolerant, so the joke was ultimately on him.

There are more common absolute questions that you'll come across in your daily life, but the point is that they are difficult to answer off the cuff, because doing so requires some indexing, thought, and decision-making. That's a lot to ask within the flow of a casual conversation. Whatever train of thought you previously had must first be derailed in order to answer this question. And then where does that leave you?

Absolute questions usually appear very innocent. For example, "What's your number-one favorite movie of all time?" That's a pretty innocuous question on its face, but it *is* an absolute question. It puts people on the spot and usually leads them to answer with, "Oh, I'm not sure, let me think about that," then never finish their thought, which of course then derails your conversation. You might as well ask them to solve an arithmetic problem. For instance:

"What's your favorite band?"

- "I don't know, let me think about that."
- "Hmm... I'm not sure. What's yours?"
- "I'll get back to you on that. I have no idea!"

The problem here is that you're asking an absolute question, which begs for an absolute answer. When you do that, you offer the other person no wiggle room and, worse, you've given them the difficult task of coming up with a definitive answer to your question. What *is* my favorite movie?

Your question will fail, the conversation will stall, and you may never get back on track. Most people like to tell the truth, and if they are tasked with something that requires them to really dig deep and come up with an honest answer to an absolute question, they will try to complete this difficult task. A small percentage of people will be able to come up with something quickly, and another small percentage of people will give a response that vaguely satisfies your question. About 1 percent of people will have these things on the tip of their tongues for whatever reason, and the rest won't know how to respond.

The bottom line: it sounds simplistic and unimportant, but using absolute statements, answers, and questions makes conversation difficult and leads to premature death. (Of the conversation, not the people involved.)

A primary rule of thumb for conversation is to make it easy for the other person, which of course makes it easy for you. Moreover, it's obvious that no one wants to carry the burden of a conversation. No one wants to fill in all the blanks, prevent all the silences, and direct the entire discussion. If your line of questioning ends up putting the burden on the other person as if it were a job interview, that other person is either going to disengage quickly, or bounce everything back to you with a "What about you?" response. Then you're going to have to deal with the mess you've created.

When you ask somebody "What's your absolute favorite (fill in the blank)?" you're putting them on the spot. You're really asking them to dig down and think, and worse, to commit to something they may not have strong feelings about. They'll likely just say the first name that pops up in their mind and pass it off as their favorite because they don't want to take too long to respond. This might be fine once or twice, but imagine how they will feel after a while if every question you ask is along similar lines.

They will start to feel as if they're at a job interview or in an interrogation instead of a pleasant social interaction. They will feel as if they're being put in a position of carrying the burden of the conversation—a responsibility they don't particularly want. It's very tiring.

So what's the solution here? Let's see how we can modify those absolute questions into questions that are far easier to answer and won't stymie people or stall the exchange.

Put boundaries around the question and make it non-absolute and people will be able to answer the question far more easily.

A common absolute question might be "What's your favorite movie?" Transform this question into:

- What are your top few movies?
- What are some good movies you've seen recently?
- Any movies you can recommend?
- Do you prefer to watch television or movies?

These questions go from more specific to broader and easier to answer. By doing this, you're not tying somebody into an absolute commitment or an absolute statement. There are several qualifiers here based on number or time, and when people don't feel pressured to come up with an absolute answer, they can relax and answer just about anything.

Moreover, open-ended questions like these give you enough material to respond well. If someone names a movie as their favorite, but you haven't seen it, you're likely headed for an awkward dead-end in the conversation. On the other hand, if someone names several movies, it gives you a better chance of being able to connect at least one of them to your own favorites and move forward with the conversation.

Here's another example. Imagine asking someone, "What's your ultimate dream vacation?" This question would likely put the person in a conundrum as to how they should answer. Do they decide based on how appealing the destination is? Do they put more weight on the place's sites or its culture? Do they need to mention time of the year, travel companions, budget considerations?

The point is, that single question touches several matters at once and would easily overwhelm the person you're talking with, especially if you're only aiming to achieve an easy, casual conversation. A key point to keep in mind is that if your question branches out to smaller points, it would do better posed in terms of its "branches" rather than imposed as an entire "tree."

So instead of expecting someone to decide on their ultimate dream vacation on the spot, consider moving your conversation along with the following more manageable prompts:

- What cool vacation places have you looked up recently?
- Any beach destinations you would recommend for a summer trip?
- Would you prefer to travel with friends or with your family?
- Would you rather go on a cruise or a road trip?

As you can see, putting boundaries around a question helps ease the pressure of giving out the "best" response among a multitude of possibilities when faced with an absolute question. Each qualifier and boundary makes the question easier to answer, and also stirs the responder's thought process to provide a more interesting and nuanced answer.

There's an additional benefit to asking people easier, more general questions. It allows them to hedge their statements in a way that makes them feel safe. There isn't an opportunity to judge taste or opinion. Some of us may never think about this, while others of us are constantly consumed by avoiding judgment.

If I were to say, "I think *Forrest Gump* is the greatest movie of all time," I imagine someone could judge me for my taste. It's a fairly black and white statement, so either you agree or disagree. It's a stance, and with each stance, there is an anti-stance.

However, if instead you said, "I saw *Forrest Gump* recently and it was pretty good," you still contribute to the topic of movies with substance, yet it's unlikely anyone will judge you unless they truly hate Tom Hanks and feel-good movies. Again, this avoidance of judgment may seem unimportant, but it is assuredly not to some people, especially those who suffer from types of social anxiety.

A good conversationalist's talent is making sure the other person is comfortable. With comfort comes openness, then comes rapport, then comes an environment ripe for witty banter. We can do this by remembering to ask broader questions that aren't looking for a right or wrong answer.

Who knows what the best movie is? This is never the point. The best questions are subjective, and your goal should be to keep conversational flow and create an environment of comfort and familiarity.

Avoiding absolute questions means sharpening your question-asking skills. It forces you to stand in the other person's shoes and see things from their (conversational) perspective. You have to take into consideration how the conversation feels from their side and not just throw out a question that happens to be stuck in your head, that ends up being extremely difficult to answer. Flow doesn't happen on accident.

Now, what if you find yourself on the receiving end of an absolute question? Should that signal the death of the conversation?

Not necessarily. You can also learn how to answer absolute questions that you're asked. We know now that absolute questions can be difficult to navigate, so you should be able to answer them more generally in a way that can contribute to flow.

Say someone asks you that question about your ultimate dream vacation. Instead of getting stumped, recall that such a question has different facets and you don't need to cover all of them in your response. You may choose to answer just one specific aspect of it, for instance by responding:

- I haven't really thought of it, but I've seen a feature on Bora Bora and it looks pretty interesting.
- Well, for this winter, some of those ski resorts seem inviting.

- Anywhere with my two best friends would be a blast!

Remember, place boundaries on your answers, and this often means answering a slightly different question than was asked. It's all too easy when you understand that people aren't seeking an accurate answer or stance, they just want to move things along.

Think Before You React

I had been talking to a coworker for about five minutes at a networking event and I was growing wearier by the second. She seemed to think our conversation was a high-stakes poker game because her face and voice were as flat as the paisley wallpaper next to her. At times, there wasn't even a blink to indicate she had heard what I said. I tried making a joke about how networking events were a human version of butt-sniffing that dogs engage in, and that didn't warrant a smile either.

To exit the conversation, I told her that I needed to visit the restroom, and I'm not sure she heard that either. Reactions are extremely important in conversation.

A conversation without reactions from the other party is like a movie without background music. At first, things seem fine, but you quickly notice that it feels empty and something is missing. You feel as if you're speaking to a wall you can't read, and one that you're not even sure is listening to what you are saying. You're not sure what to feel and how to proceed, because there are no cues given.

Reactions show people that you are more than just physically present; you are emotionally and intellectually present. If you match the energy of the person you're talking to, you'll also make them feel like you understand them better than you actually do.

As with many things, reactions have a cumulative effect. If during a five-minute conversation, the other person does not react to one or two statements you make, you might not notice. But suppose that person doesn't respond ten times in a row to something you've said? Wouldn't you start to feel anxious, as if you've said the wrong thing and they are punishing you with their complete lack of reaction?

There are a few different levels to reactions that make it clear you are listening and present.

It can be something as simple as raising your eyebrow and saying, "Oh," or even just nodding. Small acknowledgements like these should not be underrated. You don't have to be an expert at reacting, or make a big show of it; you just need to let the other person know you're engaged.

Even so, there are a few ways you can tune your reactions so that people feel a sense of conversational flow with you.

The first element is to make sure you react with the appropriate emotion. Imagine that you tell a story about breaking your arm, and the other person reacts with anger. Was that the reaction that you wanted (or expected) to receive?

No, you probably shared that story because it was either funny or pitiful (or both). Depending on the tone of your story, you were either looking for a laugh or sympathy or a little of both. "Wow, that really sucks," or "Wow, that's hilarious, but it sucks too."

Anger as a response to your story just wouldn't make sense. The easiest way to make sure you react appropriately to a story, statement, or question is to take a step back and ask yourself, "What is the primary emotion being shared here?" *and then give that back to them*!

Keep in mind that the intensity of your emotion matters as well. To use the same example, if you were to say, "Wow, I can't imagine what I'd do in your position," you might just be overdoing the sympathetic reaction. On the other hand, if you say, "That's got to be inconvenient," you're probably not being sympathetic enough, which can make the other person feel like you're undermining their emotions. As such, once you recognize the emotion they're looking for, take care to also return it in equal measure as they expressed it to you.

Here's a tip: the vast majority of emotions people share and want reciprocal, congruent reactions to are: joy, annoyance, anger, sadness, humor. Note that three out of five are negative.

For example, "Did I tell you about how this guy cut me off in traffic earlier today?!" That's a combination of annoyance and anger.

This is something that becomes instinctual and nearly instantaneous after a little bit of practice. Just think, "What emotion do they want?" What you're really trying to determine is what emotion *they* feel so you can respond in kind. When your responses accurately fit what the other person is saying (and feeling), it tells them you understand them—that you can walk a mile in their shoes. You create a lot of subconscious comfort when you react in a way that accurately corresponds to their feelings.

To reinforce such expression of understanding to the person you're talking with, take it up a notch by also mimicking their facial expression and gestures. Psychological research has shown that mirroring, a technique that involves subtly copying the other person's body language during an interaction, facilitates liking. So in responding to that person's story of being cut off in traffic, make sure you not only verbally express your annoyance, but also show it in the furrowing of your brows or the twisting of your mouth to one side.

The second way to make your reactions great is to react just a little slower than you think you should. In general, a strong reaction is better than no reaction at all. If you are stone-faced and unreactive, people feel as if they are speaking to a wall.

But reacting too quickly can impart a similar frustration. The other person may feel you are just patronizing them and are not truly interested in what they have to say. Imagine a scenario where you are excited to share something about your weekend. The person you are sharing with is nodding vigorously the whole time you're telling your story. In fact, they are almost interrupting you with their excitement. Right after you share something, they exclaim, "I know!" or "Yeah, totally! I get it!"

At some point, it becomes pretty clear that there is no way they could have processed what you said that quickly; they are just acting with fake enthusiasm because that's what they think they should do.

Did they even hear what you said amidst all that nodding and exclaiming? Because they reacted too quickly, you assume they only listened for a few "trigger words" and were answering out of reflex or habit, not in response to your actual words.

If you react too quickly, no matter your reasons for doing so, it makes you look dismissive. It makes the person you're speaking with feel as if you're not truly hearing them. You can say "I get it" all you want, but the message is that you *don't* get it and you're just trying to get them to stop talking.

That's not a great way to build mutual comfort in a conversation. When you react too quickly, it also makes people feel rushed.

If you constantly bob your head and say, "Yes, yes, yes, I get it," they feel tremendous pressure to speak quickly and finish up what they're saying. From their perspective, it is as if you're saying you're bored and already know the conclusion, so hurry it up already!

In turn, most polite people don't want to bore you. They also don't want you to feel as if you're waiting too long for your turn to speak. So they'll rush, stumble over words and likely, though perhaps unconsciously, feel annoyed.

Whatever the case, you end up creating a serious disincentive for them to freely express themselves and feel comfortable doing it. Instead, they feel they're caught in a race and have to speak really quickly and be done with it because you are waiting for your turn to contribute.

If you have a problem with reacting too quickly or overreacting, try the two-second rule. Wait two seconds after the person is done speaking before you say anything. It makes it look as if you are processing and considering what they've just said. Moreover, people are likely to perceive you as smarter if you take a few moments to respond.

You say you don't know what to do or think about during those two seconds? Well, how about what was just said and how it relates to you? And how it relates to the rest of the conversation in general? Throw on a thoughtful face, rest your hand on your chin, and people will never question your engagement again.

In summary, you don't want to overreact, nor do you want to react too quickly.

Practice Free Association

There are times when it doesn't really matter how good a speaker you are, or how interesting or engaging you might be as a person—or for that matter, how interesting and engaging the person you are speaking to is. Sometimes conversations just get stuck. It's no one's fault; it just happens.

We can get stuck in topics we don't care about, or a conversation can turn into what feels like an interview, making it feel shallow and awkward. We might discover that we have very little in common with the other person. When we try to think of different things to talk about, it becomes difficult, like trying to climb out of a hole.

When we find ourselves in a conversation where we're tangled up in a tough or impossible topic, we end up feeling frozen and trapped, which creates anxiety and frustration. The more we try to get out of the rut of the conversation, the more stuck we feel.

So let's simplify conversation.

Conversation is a series of statements, stories, and questions. After one person contributes one of those elements, the other person responds in kind, either on the same exact topic, or a topic that is in some way related to the original one.

That's where free association comes in. This is the practice wherein you say things that immediately come to mind when you hear something without trying to filter it in any way.

Isn't conversation just a series of free-association exercises?

For example, if someone says something to the effect of, "I love cats soooo much!" and you know nothing about cats, you might find it difficult to contribute anything to the conversation. If you absolutely hate cats because a cat blinded your right eye when you were a child, this might just be a conversation killer, or it might launch you into a bitter rant that will also murder the conversation.

You might not have anything to say about cats, but what if you took away the statement and context and focused on the word and concept of cats?

With simple free association, you can find a way to quickly and efficiently breathe new life into the conversation, regardless of how deeply stuck it may feel.

Just free associate five things about cats. In other words, blurt out five things (nouns, locations, concepts, statements, feelings, words) that flashed into your brain when you heard the word "cats." Allow your mind to go blank and zero in on the word "cats." Stop thinking of the word "cats" as a trigger to past experiences and memory. Instead, start looking at it as a fresh concept unconnected to what you've experienced before. Play a word association game with yourself. What does "cats" make you think of? We're just talking about purely intellectual connections.

It doesn't matter what you feel, what your emotions are. It doesn't matter what your experiences were, whether you were traumatized or not. It has nothing to do with that. This is just a purely intellectual challenge to try to rapidly fill out a list of what "cats" as a concept can be tied to.

For most people, when the word "cats" is mentioned, they think of kittens, cuddles, sand boxes, cheetahs, lions, fish, sushi, fur, dogs, allergies, the musical, etc. Keep in mind that there is no right or wrong answer here. It's all free association. What's important is that you're rapidly filling out that list of things that you can intellectually connect with the word "cats."

You'll notice that doing this is much easier than coming up with a responsive statement or question to the declaration, "I love cats sooo much." Yet, your task and challenge is exactly the same—where do you go with what the other person said? With that framework and perspective, it's much easier to disassociate from the actual statement and free associate with the subject matter.

Doing this will train your brain to think outside the (cat) box, approach conversation in a non-linear way, and see the many possible directions one simple concept or word can take you.

For instance, you may respond to the statement, "I love cats sooo much" with any of the following replies:

"I've always wondered whether cats enjoy cuddle time as much as dogs seem to do."

"Have you heard of these hypoallergenic cat breeds?"

"So would *Cats, the Musical* be something you'd enjoy watching?"

Now suppose that someone proclaimed their love for car racing, and suppose that you know nothing about that either. What are the top five or six free associations that come to mind for car racing?

For me, it's a mixture of (1) NASCAR, (2) gas, (3) tires, (4) *The Fast and the Furious* movies, (5) Japan (don't ask me), (6) Mustangs. Here's the magic part—each of these six associations are perfectly normal topics to switch to that are still in the flow of the conversation.

"I love watching car racing! It's so fun!"

"You mean like NASCAR, or illegal street racing?"

"I always wondered what kind of gas mileage those cars get."

"Do those cars have specialized tires? I don't think my car's tires could take that!"

"So are *The Fast and the Furious* movies your favorites?"

"I heard they do some kind of drift racing in Japan—do you mean like that?"

"I always imagine car racing happens with huge, powerful Mustangs. Is that the kind of car races you watch?

Try free association with the words "coffee" and "trains" and think about how much easier it is to construct questions and generally converse about something once you can form a mental map of the subject and its related topics.

You just feel *unstuck*.

Of course, the best way to do this is not to try it the first time when you're in an actual conversation. Free associating is the easy part, but utilizing the things that come to your mind in an ongoing conversation can sometimes be tricky. Practice free association consciously several times throughout the course of a week. The more you do it, the better you get at it.

Here's how to practice: on a piece of paper, write five random words. They can be anything—a noun, verb, memory, or even an emotion or feeling. Suppose the first word you write is "napkin." As quickly as possible, write three associations for that word. Take the last word you came up with, and then as quickly as possible, write three associations for that new word. Repeat three times, and then move to the next set of words.

Napkin -> table, spoon, fine dining.
Fine dining -> France, Michelin Star, butler.
Butler -> Jeeves, white gloves, Michael Jackson.
And so on.

Practicing free association is an excellent foundation for good conversation because conversation is about relating unrelated ideas, making connections, and going with the flow of topics. Next time you're struggling for something to say, take a step back and tap into your previously practiced free-association skills.

Just as with anything else that has to do with conversation skills, you can only master it if you try it enough times. The best part of all this is that you can do it instantly. You get caught in a stream of consciousness flow. Always remember there is no right or wrong answer. If you believe there is, you'll be putting unnecessary pressure on yourself.

In case you find yourself in a hole with the free-association technique for any reason, one alternative you can fall back on is to simply ask the other person to elaborate about what they said. So if someone claims to love cats or racing, nudge them to speak more about it. This will give you more material to work and free associate with. For example, common reasons for liking cats include them being cute and independent compared to dogs. If someone cites these reasons, you now have more things to free associate from—cats, cuteness, and independence. Use this abundance to come up with good responses. Flow achieved; silence averted.

Use Double Explanations

During a typical conversation, certain patterns arise.

It really boils down to the first ten questions you will probably answer when you meet someone new. By keeping these questions in mind and strategically selecting your answers, your conversations can be more satisfying and you can take advantage of these patterns by making them work for you.

At the very least, you will be able to extend the life of a typical conversation. Know these patterns and come up with distinct ways to draw out more answers, extend the conversation, and otherwise pack more perceived value into the exchange.

Regardless of who and where you meet someone, I can tell you the first ten questions and topics that will likely come up. These first ten questions can set you on a path toward flow, or they can set the tone for stagnancy and boredom.

Usually, it goes like this: How are you? How was your weekend? Where are you from? Where did you go to school? Do you have siblings? What do you do? What did you study?

It's important to enter any conversation with fully prepared answers for these common questions. If you let these small opportunities pass, you end up with boring and unengaging answers. Think of these questions as invitations to say something interesting.

By preparing for them, you can come up with an answer that will engage people while still answering the question. You come off as creative and interesting because you are ready with something unexpected to say. That's where double answers, as the section title implies, come in.

The first step is to come up with an interesting answer for the questions you know you'll be asked. But keep your answer short and simple—a "layman's" explanation. Your goal is to give information in an interesting and unique way.

For example, when somebody asks, "What do you do?" a dry, boring answer is, "I'm a lawyer." Instead, your answer should be something short and pithy like, "I file paperwork for a living," or "I'm paid to argue with people." The first path will probably not lead to intrigued questions, while the second path will certainly require closer examination, and that's just what you want. That's flow.

You get people curious. You get them to open up about what you have to say, and then you can proceed with the double explanation. To come up with powerful double explanations to common questions, start by constructing layman's explanations for each question you know you will be asked.

Again, a layman's explanation is simple, provides context, is unexpected, and draws people in. It prompts people to be interested in what you're saying.

It gives you an opening to further explain yourself, and it overall lays a far wider net or funnel to engage people. You stay general enough so that you can reach the most people, but specific enough so that you're not boring or without substance.

The layman's explanations are the first step to a double explanation. The second step involves the expert explanation. Expert explanations are what you offer once you've drawn people in with your simplified or layman's take on the topic. It's the second layer that you should have prepared for moments when it appears that someone wants to engage you further on the same topic.

This explanation draws their attention. Now that you've hooked the other party, it opens the conversation to deeper levels of engagement.

This also comes in handy when you run into somebody who actually understands the context of your answer. For example, at a dinner party, the other person might actually be a fellow attorney. When you say, "I file paperwork for a living, " she might respond with, "So do I, that's a big part of my job," and then it turns out that she's also a lawyer. The other party will quickly grasp your layman's explanation and ask you for a deeper explanation, which you will have prepared beforehand.

Essentially, the layman's explanation is an introduction, and the expert explanation is a deeper look to reveal more, if you're prompted to do so.

Following the example above, a good "expert explanation" would be, "Well I'm a corporate lawyer and specialize in business transactions and corporate filing. Lots of corporation creation, and also some investments and loan documents."

Always have these double explanations prepared. Lead with a layman's explanation because these make you look interesting, and prevent you from missing a chance to make an impression. They make you appear witty, and they open the conversation to deeper levels of engagement. However, ensure that your responses do not seem rehearsed. It can be fairly easy to spot someone who is mechanically repeating lines they've rote learned, so pause for a moment or two before replying.

Here's another example:

A layman's answer to the question of "What did you do last weekend?" could be, "I went skiing, and generally flattened the snow a lot with my butt from falling." This question can go either way. The person can say, "Well, that's awesome" and then move on to another topic, or they can choose to talk about finer details of skiing.

If you notice that this person is asking for more details, is themselves a skier, or is genuinely drawn in by your opening statement, you can offer the expert explanation.

"Oh I went on two Black Diamonds, one

Blue Diamond and got fitted for new ski poles because my old ones were bent from going over moguls." These terms will only make sense to somebody who goes skiing a lot. This will let the other person know that you know what you're talking about, and that you share their same interests.

At the same time, you don't want to appear as if you're throwing around a lot of big words just because you can. It's a surefire way of being perceived as arrogant. If you sense that the other person is interested but not someone who skis, simplify your expert explanation so that it's easily understandable for them.

Once you know the conversation won't remain superficial, you can unleash your expert explanation on people to create engagement and immediately capitalize on a common interest.

The bottom line is that by preparing beforehand, you can make conversations take a life of their own. And the good news is, as I have mentioned, conversations often involve questions that aren't all that new. They're very predictable. If you were to boil down all your conversations, they could be summed up in about ten questions, so it's easy to prepare.

By being aware of the most common questions and coming up with maybe three interesting stories or opening lines for each, you'll go a long way in becoming a better conversationalist.

More Effective Compliments

Compliments can help your conversations last longer and make you the object of someone's attention and affection. The trick is you need to know how to use them properly.

I recall once when I was a child, I was complimented on my hair and eyes by a substitute teacher looking to make conversation. The only reason I remember it is because it was clear that the substitute was trying to make a good impression on me, so she kept complimenting me on the same things every time she saw me.

Every time I came into the room from recess, every time I walked in into class in the morning, every time I came back from the bathroom... even as a child I knew something was weird.

Unfortunately, a lot of people think that compliments are like candy. They believe the more candy they give out, the more other people will like them.

That is, until the inevitable sugar rush crash or cavity. More is not always better.

On paper, compliments are great things, but if you use them improperly or in the wrong context, whatever good they can produce is flushed down the toilet. The substitute teacher from my youth took all of the goodwill she had with me and promptly flushed it down the toilet because it felt so unnatural and forced to be complimented so much.

Compliments are universally thought of as

good things, but sometimes they can make you look untrustworthy or like a flatterer. Compliments from someone who gives them out easily and frequently have little value. However, if you're perceived as the kind of person who compliments or appreciates things only when he genuinely sees value in them, your words will carry much more meaning.

As I've said often in this book, your main objective is to ensure that both of you develop a mutual comfort and confidence. A ham-fisted compliment doesn't help create that effect.

When was the last time somebody complimented you? What did you feel when you heard the compliment?

It feels good to be told that you're doing something right, or you have some redeeming value. People like to feel validated and appreciated. Paying compliments can go a long way in producing these feelings. In conversations, compliments create an air of positivity, which can boost the overall level of comfort people have with you. A properly paid compliment can go a long way in making you look good in other people's eyes.

This is not only in your mind. You start breathing a certain way. Your blood starts pumping a certain way. There is a correlation between your emotional state and physical response. The reverse is also true. When somebody says something positive to you, your brain produces neurotransmitters that are associated with a sense of well-being and happiness.

If, for example, one of your friends constantly compliments you and never fails to make you feel better about yourself, you probably start looking forward to seeing that person. You might not be able to put your finger on it, but you just want to be around him or her. What has actually happened is that your brain has paired this friend with the positive feeling of being complimented, thus creating an automatic reaction of feeling good every time you're with that person. Eventually, this positive conditioning becomes somewhat addictive.

When you're around people who constantly make you feel good, you want to be around them more often. The flip side is also true. If you come across people that are predictably negative and put you in a bad place mentally and emotionally, your tendency is to run away from them. See, conditioning also works in such a way that your brain comes to pair certain people with negative emotions, making you instantly feel ill at ease when they're around.

One of the fundamental rules of likability and charisma is the concept of reciprocity. Put simply, we are kind to people who are kind to us first. Rarely do you see somebody who reacts very negatively when somebody gives them a gift or dresses their wounds or otherwise helps them.

It is a nearly universal trait. Reciprocity is in play; when you compliment somebody, they feel good, and they feel benefited by your act. They will then look for an opportunity to repay you for your positive act by complimenting you back.

This reciprocity creates a pleasant interaction and increases the level of comfort you have with each other.

However, it's easy to get caught up in the benefits of complimenting and assume that just because you compliment people they will automatically get what you mean. You end up feeling entitled to a certain "return" for the compliments you dish out. It doesn't work that way, as my substitute teacher learned.

You have to compliment the right way, or your compliments will at best fall flat and at worst seem disingenuous. Instead of getting people to drop their guard, people will become suspicious or skeptical of your motives. You end up producing the exact opposite effect that you intended.

The first thing you need to focus on is *what* to compliment other people on.

You have to choose things to praise others for that will have the greatest impact. In other words, it has to be something that they actually care about. Otherwise, your compliment will come off as less than genuine, and you will give the impression that you're fake or manipulative.

That's the first rule of thumb. You want your compliments to have maximum effect. You want them to affect people the right way.

Here are the two key areas that are important as far as the focus of your compliments goes: things people have control over, and things people have made conscious and specific choices about.

You should compliment people on the things they can control like their clothing, fashion style, hairstyle, and living space.

While these seem like just superficial, material elements, they are also personal and impactful. Why? Because these things reflect who a person is and what they've done, whereas complimenting them on something they don't have control over, such as their eye color, doesn't.

The person has actual control over the things I listed, and they've made a choice. They've chosen their personal fashion style, their haircut, and the way they've decorated their house or flat. These things reflect a person's tastes and values.

Take wardrobe for example—people dress a certain way because they have definite values. How they dress also reflects their habits and how they'd like to be seen in the world.

Choose things that they've obviously put some thought into. This might include a bright shirt, a distinctive handbag, an unusual piece of art, or a vintage car. These are characteristics that are out of the ordinary, uncommon, and that reflect a deliberate deviation from the norm. However, if you have to choose from many things to compliment someone about, pick the one that is least obvious. Say your girlfriend dresses up for you on an occasion. She wears a fancy dress, styles her hair, and puts on nice shoes. Which one do you compliment?

Go with the least obvious one, say her earrings. It can sometimes be easy to compliment the obvious, but appreciating the things that go unnoticed makes people feel extra special because it tells them that you took the time and effort to pay close attention to them.

What makes these compliments effective is that these kinds of personal statements are what make the person feel unique.

For example, imagine I prefer Hawaiian shirts. I always show up wearing one. I obviously think highly of Hawaiian shirts, and I somehow, someway, believe they make me look different from the crowd. If I am complimented on my Hawaiian shirts, it's just confirmation that others see my train of thought and also see me as unique and interesting.

In other words, a lot of my persona and personhood are ingrained in the fact that I choose to wear these types of shirts. By complimenting someone on something they've clearly chosen with purpose, you acknowledge and validate the statement they have chosen to make about themselves. You go out of your way to let them feel special.

How do you tell what has special meaning to a person? Focus on how much time and effort are normally involved in these decisions. Somebody's political position is not something they take lightly. It's something that probably took a lot of time and consideration to develop. Often their political position is a product of their experience. Though it might be awkward to directly compliment a political viewpoint, you can try and find areas of agreement between their perspective and your own to validate them. This will show them that you're open-minded and accepting of contrasting viewpoints.

When you compliment things that reflect

individual choices, your compliment can have quite an impact.

Other characteristics you can compliment people about are their manners, the way they phrase certain ideas, their opinions, their worldview, and their perspective.

You're saying "I agree with the choices that you've made and I understand your train of thought!" The converse would be complimenting someone on something they have zero control over, such as their height.

It's nice to hear, but it ultimately amounts to "Hey, good job getting lucky in the genes department," which doesn't create much of an impact. Remember, it's not something they worked for or made a choice about. Unless you're complimenting their eyelash extensions or the shape of their eyebrows, which of course take effort to achieve, the compliment doesn't really go that far.

Since it's highly likely that a person has heard somebody else get complimented about their eyes, they won't feel particularly special if they receive a compliment about their own eyes. And, if their eyes really are notable, they've probably heard it a thousand times themselves, so you haven't offered anything different.

Your compliments have to zero in on something that provides a measure of validation. For instance, an unusual hairstyle that makes them feel special and unique. By directing your compliment there, you highlight their own self-perceived sense of how special they truly are.

When you compliment somebody's eyes or any feature they can't control, like their height, it seems generic because there are lots of people on this planet who have bright, attractive eyes.

It's not special, they've heard it before, and you could conceivably give that same compliment to fifty people that very day. There's no ownership over it. Likewise, there are lots of people who are tall. What does saying "You're so tall, it's great!" really mean to someone?

If somebody has two arms and two legs, that's not much of a compliment. In contrast, if somebody obviously works out and is suddenly wearing tighter T-shirts, that can be a tremendous source of pride for them.

Why? They put in a lot of work. They changed their normal physique from beer belly to cut and well-defined. They've made a proactive, deliberate attempt to achieve that physique—they *care*. If you truly want to maximize the effect and impact of your compliment, it all starts with being observant about other people.

Pay attention to how you think they want to be perceived, because that will give you some insight into their insecurities, and you can use your compliments to build their confidence in those areas. If someone constantly goes to the gym and makes fitness a large part of their lifestyle, it's pretty certain they want to be perceived as fit, active, and invested in health. Call that out with a compliment.

Compliments that target things the person has put great effort into will pay huge dividends. This formula pays off like clockwork.

Takeaways

- You know those people who always have something clever or witty to say? Ever wonder how they cultivated this seemingly magical quality? If you have, know that being witty is much easier than you might think, and you don't have to be born with the gift of gab. By following certain tricks and techniques, you can develop the same persona yourself. The first element to tackle is conversational flow and keeping a back and forth going.
- The first trick in the book is to never speak in absolutes. Eliminate questions and statements involving words like favorite, absolute, only,

worst, etc., from your vocabulary. If you ask someone "what's your absolute favorite movie?", you are actually asking a pressurized question that introduces pause and destroys flow. Instead, always generalize your questions by putting boundaries and constraints on them. This doesn't require as much thought from your conversational partner, allowing them to simply answer a question with a range of responses instead of being caught looking for the one "right" answer.

- Reactions are important. People say and do things for a reason, and it's usually to get a reaction. This step is deceptively simple yet difficult. Pay attention to other people and ask yourself what emotion they want to evoke. Then give it to them. Don't take too long to reply, but being too quick isn't advisable either. This is all to make others feel that you are present and engaged.

- If your mind goes blank, use a technique called free association to generate a response. These are words that immediately come to mind upon hearing something. For example, if someone talks about cats, practice free association with the provided exercises, and you'll be able to come up with answers more quickly and easily. Conversation as a whole is just a series of interrelated responses and stories, so free association is practicing conversation flow.

- Regardless of who you're talking to, you're likely to be asked the same set of generic questions. These include what do you do, how was your day, and others like these. You'll want to have two separate answers prepared for such questions, one of which is interesting and unique (the layman explanation), while the other is more informative (the expert explanation). Being too esoteric upon first meeting someone isn't always helpful, and can confuse and render others speechless.

- Finally, learn to give good compliments. This is also deceptively easy. Compliment things that people have control over, or made a choice about. Don't choose genetic qualities like height or eye color; instead choose things that people actively put effort into. People feel comfortable and flattered, and then start to open up.

Chapter 2. Conversation Is Play

Now that we've gone over some techniques for achieving a kind of conversational flow, or at least avoiding awkward silences, let's dive into some ways that we can simply play and enjoy ourselves more in social interaction. Many times, there are high expectations and a pressure to present yourself in a certain way. But this robs us of one of the major benefits of conversation—play and amusement. The distinction may seem small, but these two goals lead to diverging paths.

Outside of a few select contexts, we should always be optimizing for play and amusement. After all, that's the point of this book. If you wanted to learn about how to navigate office politics, you might be looking at the wrong text.

Break the Fourth Wall

The fourth wall is a term in television, movies, and plays where the character steps out of his role and addresses the audience directly. Think of it as an actor being surrounded by three walls on the stage. There are, of course, the back wall and the two side walls. The fourth wall is the space directly in front of the actor. When the actor speaks directly to the audience, he is breaking the fourth wall.

If you've ever seen *Ferris Bueller's Day Off* with Matthew Broderick, he breaks the fourth wall constantly by addressing the audience as if he is aware that he is being watched. Another example is Kevin Spacey in *House of Cards.* He would directly address his audience either through words, or just simple expressions to convey how he really felt. And of course, who could forget Jim Halpert from *The Office* and his bewildered looks toward the camera?

When you break the fourth wall, you are subtly acknowledging something about the conversation at hand that you are presently participating in.

Imagine that your conversation is a television show in which you are both characters and you are reading your lines from a script. To break the fourth wall would mean stepping out of the conversation and making an observation about the discussion or topic or something else concerning the context of the conversation. You can also refer to this as being "meta" about the current conversation.

You are breaking the fourth wall of the conversation by commenting on the conversation itself in an observational or analytic way. You are speaking as if you were studying it from the outside.

For example:

- "Wow, this conversation has really taken an odd turn, hasn't it?"

- "Did you just make a reference to the Spice Girls and '90s boy bands?"
- "We got so distracted that we were walking in the mud!"
- "I apologize in advance for talking too much about coffee."

Breaking the fourth wall is a comment on the conversation itself and is observational. It is best delivered with a bit of surprise and curiosity, because the context is that you are so moved in a good way that you were compelled to comment. You had to break character and comment where it was due. If you do it right, breaking the fourth wall shows a higher level of self-awareness.

It calls attention to something that you noticed about the other person, and in most cases, it's something the other person did consciously or was proud of. With the above example, it's very likely that someone consciously made a reference to a '90s boy band because they thought it was entertaining—they'd be very glad to know that you also thought so.

This tactic also tells the other person that you are paying attention to what's happening at a deeper level of the conversation.

Just as with other techniques I've covered in this book, don't overdo it. In many cases, people are in such a rush to try to look smarter than they actually are that they end up using the fourth wall in a disastrous way. This will result in your attempt coming across as forced and overly self-conscious, which will only make the other person choose their words more carefully around you out of fear of being misinterpreted.

On that note, you shouldn't comment negatively or doubtfully because that will come off as particularly judgmental and as if you are looking down on the other person. For example, breaking the fourth wall to say something like "Did you really just make a comment on holistic medicine?" would likely appear as an attack. This is in contrast with breaking the fourth wall positively, which in effect is praising the other person for something.

Instead of getting both parties in the conversation to laugh at the conversation, or at least feel a tremendous amount of comfort, breaking the fourth wall negatively makes you end up looking patronizing, condescending, or downright insulting. These effects are the mirror opposite of what you are trying to achieve and do not help you.

Bad example: "Are you really directing the conversation toward yourself again?"

Bad example: "Just a side note, I think it's funny that you were the butt of that joke."

In both cases, Breaking the fourth wall to say something negative lends the impression that you were especially offended by something, while doing it for something positive results in the opposite outcome.

So when do you use it? Here are two easy occasions and contexts where you can break the fourth wall with a strong, positive impact.

First, this technique can be used to point out what both people are thinking but not saying. This can be related to your surroundings, or something notable from the conversation itself.

"Did we just talk about toilet brands for ten minutes? We definitely are a good match."

"Wow, we just walked by a sixty-year-old Michael Jackson impersonator, didn't we?"

Second, you can use the fourth wall conversation tactic to point out your opinion on the conversation or what is happening at the moment. Make sure that your opinion, however, is positive, entertaining, or preferably both.

If the conversation has progressed to loud laughing and vigorous fist-pumping, then you might comment, "This conversation has really escalated, hasn't it?"

Conversely, if you are confused about where the conversation topic is going, you might say, "Frankly, I have no idea where this conversation is headed, but I like it."

The "Us Against the World" Technique

People like to feel as if they belong. It's a universal desire. Regardless of what culture we come from, regardless of what geographic region we are from, we all like to feel as if we're part of a greater collective.

Some of us need to feel we're part of a greater global ecosystem and others just want to feel included and accepted by their soccer team, or even just the person they're talking to. This is a tremendous psychological reservoir you can tap into to help you become a better conversationalist.

Granted, that's a pretty high and lofty description for the simple "us against the world" technique, but it accomplishes all those things at once in someone's mind.

What does the technique look like?

Simple: "Boy, it is really loud in there. Can you believe all these people getting deaf in there?"

It doesn't seem like much, but it's quick and effective.

That statement creates an in-group that is special and separate from the rest of the room or world. You've essentially created your own group that contains the two of you—the two of you possess special knowledge, share the same thoughts, are above the rest of the people milling about and damaging their eardrums, and are essentially the only two sane people. It's you two against the rest of the world, which has gone *crazy*. In a sense, you're breaking the fourth wall here as well, because you are commenting on a situation that you are inside, from the outside.

It's the same feeling when you witness something incredibly odd, and you and a stranger lock eyes and exchange knowing glances. You're calling out a commonality in thought process or current environment and making it clear that only you two have that commonality. When you comment to them out loud, you make it clear that you view them as being on the same level of understanding and train of thought as you. And whether or not they agree, they will feel inclined to agree and join your in-group.

"Us against the world" is an especially helpful tactic when you're in some way "forced" to stay with an acquaintance or even a complete stranger in certain situations. How many times have you attended a party which had you stuck with a friend's friend at a table, with no one else but the two of you silently munching on your snacks? Unless you have the conversational skills to remedy it, this situation easily disintegrates into an awkward dance of eyeballs avoiding contact with one another and the occasional dry smile while silently praying for your friend's return at the soonest time possible.

The next time you find yourself in such a position, try this technique as a conversation starter. Voice out an observation about the event you're both in, the food that's served, or the general behavior of the people around you. Doing so will be an open invitation to the other person to also present their opinion or observation on what you have just pointed out, acting like a spark on wood to ignite a conversation.

Ideally, point out something which you are fairly certain the two of you have in common, or something both of you share in contrast with the rest of the world (who don't possess this characteristic). Here's how such a chat might go:

"Hey, have you noticed how the tables around us have piled on greens on their plates while we both went for meats aplenty?"

"Yeah. I'm a big carnivore."

"Me too. Though I once tried going vegan several years back."

"Really? How was it?"

"Let's just say I had a cow."

As such example showed, the initial comment made about food choices at a party became a springboard for sharing preferences and experiences about food and eating habits in general. The conversation would likely blossom as each person could continue sharing more about their own eating habits and interesting food experiences.

Another way to think about it is that you have created your own inside joke. When you are truly part of an in-group that consists of two people, you have unique, exclusive shared experiences that you can talk about at a later point. "Hey, remember when we met and our eardrums almost blew out?"

As you can see, using the "us against the world" technique can be subtle and easy. But it's also easy to miss the mark. And if you miss the mark, you will sound as if you're just making an observation about something obvious with no good reason to do so.

It turns a proper usage of the technique, like, "Can you believe the types of awkward small talk people are trying here?" into "Yeah, these events are awkward."

What you need to do is take stock of how you can create an in-group with someone. Generally, you want to observe (1) what is noteworthy at the moment to comment on, (2) what you share in common contextually and not personally, and (3) general emotions that you probably share based on the context.

For noteworthy things to comment on, you might say "Yeah, I saw that Michael Jackson lookalike too and feel like I'm going crazy. Same with you?"

For sharing a common context, you might say "Can you believe how aggressive everyone is here? It's a bit much!"

For general emotions that you probably share, you might say "Glad I'm not the only one here who..." or "Yeah, it's exhausting in there, isn't it?"

When you use the "us versus the world" conversation technique, it allows you to draw on similarities you may have with the person you are speaking with. It also teases out similar thought patterns that both of you may share. You do this by simply recognizing and highlighting them. In reality, you two probably aren't different from everyone else in that geographic space or context, but your comments can make it seem as if you are.

By calling out this perceived similarity, you openly create a feeling of closeness and kinship. At least, the other person thinks you are thinking along the same lines, and on the same level, as they are. In some cases, you'll also be able to use this technique non-verbally. Simply gesturing toward something odd with your head or eyes and laughing about it establishes the same bond. This can be particularly useful in loud places or where the person you're trying to gesture to is sitting far away from you, like at a large table.

This technique is tremendously helpful because the number-one rule in likability is to make people feel that you are like them. Regardless of skin color, religious, ethnic, and other differences, we prefer people who are similar to us at some level.

This taps into that psychological reservoir I mentioned in the beginning of this chapter. We'd like to create a psychological "safe spot" for us and people similar to us. These are our friends; these are people we can rely on, and people we can trust.

This is such a deep and profound psychological truth for human beings because it's hard-wired into our DNA. Imagine yourself on an African savannah

50,000 years ago. Imagine walking through that grassland and having an "Us versus the World" mindset.

With that mindset in operation, you could identify allies that would help your family or tribe members stay alive. Now, imagine the opposite situation. Think of what would happen if you didn't think that way. You'd probably end up as lunch to a local lion.

Use this basic psychological truth to your advantage by creating a perception of similarity. The reality is that you and your conversational partner aren't really all that different from the rest of the people around you. But by using this technique, you create an artificial feeling of closeness and similarity that leads to a higher level of likability.

It also creates the impression that you are an observant person. It makes you look observant enough to notice these things and call them out. And this is why you and the person you're speaking to are on the same wavelength. Where does this all lead to? Well, it leads to the other party being encouraged to further share their thoughts with you. They feel they belong, and that feeling creates a higher degree of comfort which pushes the conversation along.

Use Fallback Stories

Fallback stories, as I like to call them, can be used as fallbacks (duh) when you run out of things to say. But they can also be used to engage people, invigorate a conversation, or get a rise and laugh out of people who feel a bit too stiff at the moment.

What makes a fallback story different from a normal story?

Well, a fallback story has four distinct components—but don't worry, they come fairly naturally and organically once you've had a tiny bit of practice with them.

I'm also not that focused on the storytelling aspect itself, as that tends to work itself out (and actually not matter too much) once you have the other components in place.

There are four components to fallback stories: (1) the bridging sentence, (2) the story itself, (3) your opinion of the story, and (4) asking for the other person's opinion in a few different ways. As I said, you will very quickly get used to this process because it is very natural.

First off, here's an example. Imagine that a conversation is dying down, or there is a lull between topics.

(1) Hey, you know what I heard recently?

(2) One of my female friends just proposed to her boyfriend, and now they are engaged. Apparently she just didn't want to keep waiting and decided to be progressive and ignore gender roles and take her life into her own hands. She even had a ring and everything.

(3) When I first heard about it, I generally thought why not, it's 2020! I know them both and it kind of suits their relationship.

(4) What do you think about that? Would you ever do that? How would you react if your significant other did that with you? Would you do the ring as well?

At first glance, this seems like a casual, attention-grabbing story that will definitely engender conversation because of the way it was presented, and the questions posed at the end to continue discussion. You need not ask all of them together, since that would be a lot to remember. Have one or two questions that you can ask as a follow-up once you've told your story. A barrage of questions might just make the other person nervous about which one they should answer first or concentrate more heavily on. Each of the separate components plays an important role, however.

The first component is the bridging sentence, and while it is short, it provides a simple, plausible transition from whatever the previous topic was into your fallback story. You don't need to say much with it, it just provides context for why you are even bringing the matter up. You just heard about it recently. Don't overthink this part with protests like "How can you dive into that topic from silence or the former topic?" That's what this bridging sentence does in an easy and quick way. "You know what I heard recently?" is a fairly flexible option, while others you can use include "Want to know something interesting that happened recently?" and "You won't believe what happened the other day." All three of these evoke some curiosity, giving you the perfect segue into your story.

The second component is the actual story itself. Now, notice that it's not long, and the story details don't even matter that much here. The story just introduces one or two main premises, and I don't go into the nitty-gritty detail because that's not what drives a conversation forward.

I introduce the premises, try to focus on the one or two primary emotions that I want to evoke, and move on from there. It's short, and most storytelling books gum it up and make it too convoluted by introducing formulas for telling a simple story. If you tell the story right, the reaction isn't about the story itself, it's about the questions it poses (and that you pose).

Another way to conceptualize an effective and snappy story is to think "What is the primary emotion and point of the story I am trying to tell?" and distill that into one sentence. If you can't, your stories are probably rambling messes that make people scream internally.

The third component is my opinion (as the speaker) on the matter. For most of these fallback stories, you want to provide a positive opinion; otherwise people may not feel comfortable opening up and sharing if they happen to disagree with you. In other words, if I said I thought it was a terrible decision that the female proposed to the male, the other person may refrain from saying they thought it was a good idea for fear of irking or contradicting me. Just share how you feel about it and try to place yourself in the context.

This component is key to opening the other

person up, because you've shared first and made yourself vulnerable. The other person will feel safer after you've disclosed your position first—that's just a facet of human psychology.

The fourth and final component seems like a series of inane questions, but there is logic to the chaos. When you ask someone to generally comment on a situation, most people have a tough time with this request because it is so open-ended and broad.

They have an infinite choice of directions to go and they aren't sure of the exact question you asked.

"Would I do that?" they might be thinking. "What do you mean? Propose at all? If I were a woman, or as a man? I don't understand the question you're asking."

Thus, fallback stories are best when concluded with a series of questions. The reason is that the type of answer you are looking for becomes clear when you ask a series of questions, and different questions will resonate with different people. So the person you're speaking to might not really understand or have anything to say about the first three questions, but will light up upon hearing the fourth question... even if it is essentially the same question posed in a different way.

The reason I know this approach with a series of questions works is because you can physically see people's faces light up when you ask a question that resonates with them and when they have something to answer with... again, even if it's the same exact question worded differently.

Those are the four components of a good fallback story—and again, the best part about these is you can prepare them beforehand and carry them up your sleeve for whenever you feel you need to spice things up conversationally.

Does the above story seem like a good one? It never fails because it's an interpersonal situation with universal themes and questions—which means that essentially everyone can have an opinion on it.

When you are thinking of what fallback stories to put up your sleeve, interpersonal situations tend to work for that reason. Other prompts that make good fallback stories include asking people what they would do in certain hypothetical situations, and asking for opinions on moral dilemmas (as long as they aren't dark and depressing).

You're going for universal themes above all else, because that's when you can ensure that people will have something to add to the ensuing discussion, otherwise it will just turn into you telling a story about an interesting occurrence.

For example:

- My friend spent $300 on a meal, mostly on wine, for no apparent occasion or reason. In what circumstances would you spend $300 on a meal?
- My friend saw his friend's significant

other cheating on his friend. He told his friend. Would you tell?

- Someone took a $40,000 pay cut to work at their dream job. Where is the line for you?
- Someone found out they had two weeks to live and went to Antarctica. Does that sound attractive to you, or would you do something completely different?

Just remember to phrase these all into stories that seem to have randomly popped into your head, provide your opinion, and ask for their opinion in various ways.

Instant Role Play

One of the best ways to break out of interview mode is to engage in role play. Taking on a character, leaving yourself behind, and engaging in the ultimate type of *conversational play*.

Let's think about that from a bird's-eye view.

You're stuck in an interview style of small-talk conversation. There doesn't seem to be any hope of transitioning into a conversation that builds any meaningful rapport. You both feel too self-conscious and restrained in what you can talk about. You feel trapped, and to make things worse, the friend who gave you a ride won't be back for another hour or so.

Now, what if you decided to act like someone from a television show or movie? What if you actively imagined what that character would do in your situation and said it out loud?

Imagine that the other person went through the same exact process, and started playing the role of someone else. What would your conversation look like at that point?

Much better!

Therein lies the magic of role playing. Not only is it great for conversational play and amusement, it can break you out of conversational prisons. It allows you to say what you might not otherwise say, and act in ways that you normally would be too self-conscious to ever do.

It is playing around and injecting a lot of fun and informality into your conversation. You don't want to be stuck in a situation where you ask a question, the other person answers, then they ask a question, and you answer. In many cases, such exchanges are superficial and forgettable.

If you want to get the attention of the person and make a good impression, play around with them and do a little bit of role play.

Instant role play is easier to do than the tactics in the previous two chapters, and will also help you infuse some humor into a conversation. The tricky part is getting the other person to play along. To be successful, choose generic roles that anyone can play with little effort.

Telling traditional jokes with their structural requirements requires the right topic and situation for them to make sense. That kills a lot of spontaneity and fun during a conversation. Until you get up to speed, it's usually a better decision to try more conversational laugh tactics, and instant role play is one of them.

Just like the scenario at the beginning of this chapter, role play takes you to a different mental arena where people use their wit and deliberately work together with you during the conversation to keep playing out those roles.

You are creating an improvised comedy performance on the fly, and with this technique, you tell people what roles they will play so they will naturally comply with you. You are the one initiating the role play, and this allows people to follow you when they see a clear direction as to where to go.

At the root of it, role playing is fun. When you get into it, people will take off running. Whether or not we did choir or theater in school, it's fun to step into someone else's life, even for a short time.

At some point in our lives, we have tried to play a role, or we say ridiculous things that we normally don't say. We try to step into the shoes of somebody else and look at the world from their perspective and act accordingly. Doing so engages many different aspects of our personal imagination and creativity. It's a great way to step out of our daily routine and roles.

Most people welcome role playing because our personal roles can get restrictive in reality. For example, your role is a son, a friend, a boyfriend, an employee, and so on and so forth. It is too easy to define yourself based on your roles instead of who you really are. As a result, most jump at the opportunity to break out of their daily lives with role playing. Think about how empowered you feel when you wear a mask during Halloween and become anonymous.

So, what are the steps in role playing?

Step one: make a "judgment" statement about someone.

The trick is that the statement has to put them in contrast to you. It has to make them relatively better, worse, funnier, happier, crazier, or calmer than you. It can be a compliment, or a playful tease, as long as it contrasts yourself to the other person.

For example, you can give them a compliment. This puts them in a superior role to you. You might say, "Your sense of style is so amazing, I wish I had it too." This statement implies that the other person has better taste in clothing than you. Relative to you, they are superior in this regard.

A tease, on the other hand, puts them in an inferior role to you. For example, when you say, "Nice jacket. Do they make it for women?" the implication is that they can't tell the difference between and men's and women's jackets, and they need help dressing themselves. Relatively speaking, you are superior to them in this regard.

You aren't judging them, but you are making a statement that assigns a value to the other person.

Step two: give them a label based on the statement that you made.

Here you'll see why it is so important that the statement you made in step one assigns a relative value.

For example, if you give somebody the compliment "Wow, you are great at navigating," continue on and give them a title or label, such as "Milwaukee's very own Magellan," or "my go-to personal GPS during road trips."

If you went the opposite way and teased someone with "you are terrible at navigating," you would give them a title or label such as "You are like Lewis and Clark but blind" or "Google Maps but offline."

It is important that you actually give them a title or label, versus just describing how good or bad they are relative to you. It's important because... *that's the role they will be playing!*

Step three: starting playing the roles!

Whatever title or label you have given them, that's the other person's role.

What is your role? This is why the role needs to be relative to you: you can either be someone who is learning from that person, or someone who is teaching that person.

For example, if someone is the *modern-day Magellan*, then that's their role, and your role is to be curious about how they learned their craft and got so good at it. If you elevate someone, then your role is inferior to them.

If someone is *Google Maps but offline*, then their role is inferior to you, and you take the role of teaching them. If you playfully tease someone down, your role is superior to them.

Spell out the roles, and then act in them. This is crucial to the humor. You have to remain consistent.

This is how it sounds all put together from top to bottom:

"You are so great with maps and navigating, I can't believe it. You're like a modern-day Magellan."

"Oh, thanks, man. I've just done it a lot."

"No, you're Magellan. Which continent did you most enjoy discovering?" (This is where you've assigned them their role, and are literally putting them into it and asking them to embrace it.)

"Oh... probably South America. The fruit is so good there." (Here, they catch on that you are role playing. Not everyone will catch on immediately, or at all. If they catch on, they will stay in character and continue with the tone you've set. If they don't happen to catch on, move on and try again in a short while.)

"Yeah, that makes sense. Did you interact

with the locals?"

"All the time!"

"Did you men enjoy the locals or the fruit more?"

"Hard to say…"

So, what happened there? I explicitly told my conversational partner their role, and it came from the title that I gave them because of a compliment. The compliment was hyperbolic and exaggerated as those are the easier types of roles and characters to play.

It's much easier—and more interesting—to play someone who is incredibly insane versus mildly disturbed, right?

After the person realizes what is happening, it's up to you to keep the role play going. You've created the roles, the situation, and you have to continue to guide it.

Here's another example of instant role play

in action:

"This roast chicken tastes heavenly. You really know your way around the kitchen. You must be the local Bobby Flay!"

"Oh yes, I used the same recipe found in my new cookbook. Have you gotten a copy of it yet?"

"Not yet. Fancy giving me a signed copy?"

"Sure! As long as you don't forget to tune in to my new show over at Food Network tomorrow evening."

"Ah yes, you're going to feature your barbecue sauce recipe there, right?"

"Yes. And if you invite me for a barbecue, I might just prepare that signature sauce for you and your other guests then!"

As you can see, instant role play is easier to instigate than you think. It allows you to blow through conversational impasses and enter a mode of thought where you are playing with the other person. It's a much better mindset for rapport, and more conducive to making friends than beginning with small talk and trying to transition from there.

Takeaways

- All of conversation is an opportunity for playful interaction. It just takes a shift in mindset to see that, and the world will open up.
- Breaking the fourth wall is a simple, yet effective move to make any conversation more interesting. Often used in movies, this technique essentially involves commenting about the conversation you're having in some positive way. This is generally something that both parties are thinking but has gone unacknowledged. If you're having a particularly funny conversation with someone, you might jokingly remark, "Things have really escalated, haven't they?" This is a great way to connect as it shows that you're aware of your

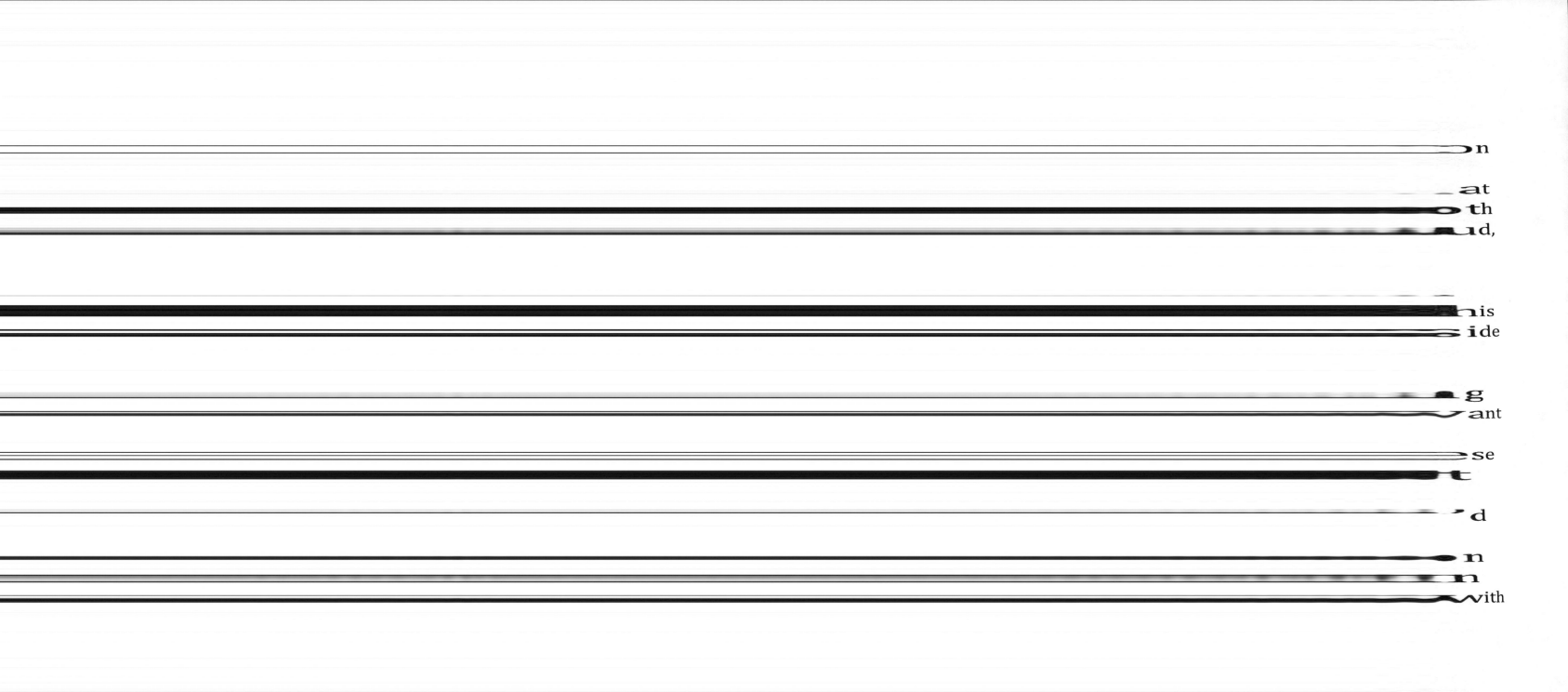

boyfr

ques t

simil

surp r

- We a l

tech n

This i

trick s

gene r

up so

them

are fo

comp l

some

being

them

being

they'll

naviga

intere

naviga

enjoy

them i

Chapter 3. A Touch of Witty Banter

What's a sure recipe for a sparkling and enjoyable conversation? Of course, a dash of witty banter! While the previous chapters have trained you in the art of keeping the dialogue flowing like a river and prepped you to approach conversation as play, this chapter will equip you with the tools to spruce up your chats with chuckles courtesy of well-timed and clever quips.

A mindset for banter is a mindset for play and entertainment. Unfortunately, it's probably not what you're used to.

Currently, you are probably taking statements and questions from people at face value, not giving it a second thought, and staying in the literal track of a conversation. As a result, things may unintentionally take on the more businesslike feeling of an interview rather than a chat with a close friend.

Here's a quick and simple illustration. If I asked someone how the weather was outside, a literal, face-value answer would be, "It just started to sprinkle. Looks cold."

An answer from someone who had a humorous mindset would be significantly different: "It's not wet enough to need an umbrella, but say goodbye to your hairdo." The difference is in how literal one would interpret the question to be, and how literal the answer given is. Sounds a little bit like the two types of explanations you can give, right?

There's a reason that some people seem to have funny quips every minute, while you might feel like you have one good retort every two weeks. The difference isn't that they're inherently funnier, it's that they have the right mindset for it. They're prepared for humor, and even hunting for it.

As you saw in the example above, most of us are stuck in the mode where we are too serious in our conversations. We think that just because they started a certain way, they need to fit a certain mold and follow that template or transcript to completion. We do this because we run on autopilot quite frequently, and we are habituated to allow opportunities slip away.

If someone asks about weather, yes, they want to know the temperature. But it doesn't stop there. You can answer the question in many ways that don't simply require you to answer it like a test question.

We have many expectations about where our conversations should go and how they should flow, but in reality, people don't care about these expectations.

What's more, these expectations often lead to conversations about things that neither party cares about. What makes this so awkward is that both parties are just too polite to say anything about the conversation. No one wants to talk about the weather for more than one sentence each.

So, how can we create a mindset where we instantly see more humor in our daily lives as a result of taking a different angle? It's playing versus discussing, or amusing versus conversing. There are many ways to look at these two different modes of thought.

The default conversation approach most people use is to, of course, discuss and converse. There's nothing wrong with that, and it can certainly lead to interesting revelations.

The problem is that it gets old quickly, and it can take on a serious and somber tone if that is your approach to a conversation. It's not the ideal way to build rapport since it can be a dry discussion of facts and news, which doesn't tell you anything about a person's personality, nor does it allow you to show your own off.

People discuss current events with

colleagues. People play around with and amuse friends with personal stories. See the difference?

The difference in mindset should be to focus on being more playful, not taking people at face value, and not worrying about answering questions literally. Just because someone asked about the weather doesn't mean that you are only allowed to talk about the weather.

How can you do this?

You may actively think about how you react to someone in a playful manner. Imagine how you would react if you were five years old, and that is truly a better approximation for playful conversation that can build rapport.

If someone asks you about the weather, what are the different ways you can reply?

You can ask silly questions, you can say things solely to see how others respond. You might create outlandish hypotheticals, you can address the elephant in the room, you can allow your inner monologue to be read out loud, and so on.

You may generally view the other person as someone to joke around with, as opposed to making a professional first impression on. You don't need to give people straight, exact answers. People are usually far more attracted to interesting and noteworthy answers. Unless you are giving an oral report, it's not a stretch to say that they would always prefer something to catch their attention versus being dry and accurate.

Remember that you're not necessarily looking to absorb or convey a set of facts, or extract certain information. Instead, your goal is simply to feel good around people and, most importantly, make them feel good around you. With this in mind, we can set the grounds for sharing witty banter.

Word of caution: be sure to actually answer someone's question. You can be both humorous and informative. Make sure to occasionally check in with the other person to make sure that you aren't going overboard with the lack of substantive content if they're seeking it.

The Witty Comeback Machine

As a former fat kid, I used to have a fairly extensive library of witty comebacks for those charming people who liked to point out that I was, indeed, fat.

Or that they couldn't ride in a car with me for fear of it tipping over.

Or that I was so big my Polo brand sport shirt had a *real* horse on it (this one was pretty clever, I'll admit).

Mind you, I wasn't really that large—just twenty pounds overweight. At some point, however, I developed one type of comeback that never failed to either shut people up, or bring them to my side through laughter.

Were you also aware that my Polo Sport shirt can be used as a parachute?

You'd better put six extra wheels on your car for me.

Watch out, I'm going to sit on you and suffocate you.

What exactly are these lines composed of, and why are they so effective?

Becoming a witty comeback machine is easier than you think, and it's one of the best conversational tactics you can learn. This technique doesn't only rear its head when dealing with insults—it is widely applicable once you learn the framework. If it's a bad situation, a witty comeback can diffuse the tension and bring emotional levels back to normal. If it's a good situation, then a witty comeback can make it even better.

Whatever the situation, mastering witty comebacks will earn you the respect of other people for your clever wit. It just takes one line—and the shorter and punchier, the better and more effective. The longer a comeback, the less the punch it carries.

A witty comeback does many things simultaneously. It makes people laugh and disarms them while allowing you to appear smart, insightful, and mentally quick. It also shows people that you're easygoing and can handle hurdles that come your way. When most people are insulted or made fun of, they either respond with anger or try to play it down. With a witty comeback, you're showing others that such remarks don't faze you nearly as much as they would someone else.

Before I get ahead of myself, let me define what a witty comeback is.

Wit is essentially spontaneous creativity. You take a topic or statement and see it from a different angle in a way that is relatable, yet novel. That's why I kind of enjoyed the aforementioned joke about the Polo Sport shirt, even if it was at my expense.

Witty comebacks can be hurtful, serious, or completely light and harmless. It all depends on you. You can be joking and playing around, or you can wield a sharp sword. You can also do both. If you're being bullied like I often was, a witty comeback can be both funny, as well as signal to others that they should back off.

What's tricky about wit is that something that may be funny and completely harmless to you can be destructive or hurtful to someone else. You have to know where that fine line is and you have to know how to straddle it. Often, it comes down to the way you respond with a comeback and the words you choose to do so. The same thing said with a serious or smiling expression will be perceived differently. Similarly, some words are more likely than others to flare tension. Delivery matters, and if you can master that, you'll be less likely to be misunderstood.

There are a few tricks to use so that you always have a witty comeback in your pocket ready for launch—instead of twenty minutes after the encounter.

First, when thinking about a witty comeback, don't think generically.

Don't use, "I know you are, but what am I?" or "So is your mom." People judge a witty comeback based on how original it is— remember, it's spontaneous creativity. Using something that is both generic and not clever is decidedly neither spontaneous nor creative. Don't just use a template-driven witty retort that you've seen in a movie or something that works better in a different context. And don't use one of the comebacks you thought were hilarious when you were ten. Those don't work anymore.

Second, don't act like you can't take a joke.

Of course, witty comebacks need an initial statement to "come back" to.

The vast majority of the time, people are indeed joking when they say something negative about you in your presence. In a sense, it's a compliment because they assume you have a sufficient sense of humor and the emotional resiliency to deal with it. The people who *aren't* involved in jokes and good-natured ribbing don't have many friends.

If you let it show that you are angry or hurt, it spoils the playful tone you could otherwise enhance with your witty comeback. Focus on the intent of the person saying the remark; they likely did not mean to hurt you, even if they accidentally ended up doing that.

For example, if someone made a joke about my fatness, and I got visibly angry, they would likely stop... then walk on eggshells around me for days. When someone is uncomfortable with something, they make others uncomfortable as well. If that happens enough times it becomes clear that I don't have a sense of humor and I let my insecurity infect my relationships. Know where to draw the line.

It's okay to be the butt of jokes sometimes, but if repeated remarks about an insecurity genuinely bother you, don't use witty comebacks to undermine your self-esteem. Though it might diffuse any tension, it will make you feel like a doormat. That's where discussion of boundaries comes into play, and banter is no longer appropriate. But that's a subject for another book.

Generally, handle the initial negative statement with a wry smirk and with the knowledge that you are about to crush them.

Third, use the right tone.

The best witty comebacks are delivered with 50 percent indifference. When you deliver one with 100 percent excitement and 0 percent indifference, guess what happens? You blow it and the comeback falls flat. Indifference is the correct tone because comebacks are about your attitude—pretend that you are James Bond delivering a witty retort after a failed murder attempt by a villain. Fifty percent indifference also ensures that you aren't being aggressive or spiteful. It's far too easy for a bit of bitterness and negativity to slip into your tone.

A witty comeback is the verbal equivalent of judo or aikido—using an opponent's words against them. If you take that analogy, you need a certain amount of cool to effectively counteract your rival. Witty comebacks take the power away from the insult hurled. However, saying something too excitedly or with the wrong tone betrays that you were affected by the remark, making it harder to appear cool or indifferent.

There are three main types of witty comebacks. None are better than the other. You just need to pick the type you're most comfortable with.

Type #1: Pick apart their words.

Think about the other person's word choice and quickly analyze whether there is another angle or meaning to those words.

An easy approach is to interpret their words as overly literal or outlandish. The key is to interpret them in a way that is favorable to you to make it seem as if they complimented you instead of put you down.

Bob: *You are working as slow as a glacier. Pick it up!*

You: [focusing on the word glacier] *You mean I'm strong and cool under pressure? True.*

Your job is made considerably easier when someone uses a simile like Bob did, but in the absence of one, you can focus on the thing they're putting you down about. To take the same example, let's say Bob said, "You're working too slowly. Pick it up!"

One way you can respond is by thinking of the benefits of working slowly, leading to a comeback like, "The tortoise always wins the race!" Not only are you calling yourself a tortoise in a playful way, but assuring Bob that your rate of work will have benefits that he would appreciate.

Type #2: Agree and amplify.

For this tactic, take your cue from the way the cartoon character SpongeBob SquarePants handled Mr. Krabs' mocking words, "That hat makes you look like a girl." Instead of feeling hurt and handing over the hat like Mr. Krabs would like, SpongeBob batted his eyelashes and said in a sweet voice, "Am I a pretty girl?"

The idea here is to agree with whatever the insult was, and then add to it in an absurd way. You amplify the initial sentiment to a degree that is ridiculous. This was my go-to technique to deflect jokes about my weight.

If you forgot from earlier in this chapter:

Were you also aware that my Polo Sport shirt can be used as a parachute?

You'd better put six extra wheels on your car for me!

For another example:

Bob: *Your cooking was pretty terrible last time.*

You: *You're lucky you didn't stay until the end of the night, we all got our stomachs pumped. Dinner at my place later tonight?*

Type #3: Use an outlandish comparison.

Actually, this is related to the prior point, and it brings the conversation into a different sphere and makes both people laugh at the weird, outlandish imagery. What makes this work is that the comparison, although extreme, is still somewhat realistic. To use the same framework, you're amplifying (to yourself or the other person) with an analogy here.

Bob: *Your cooking was pretty terrible last time.*

You: *True, I should have used the eggs as hockey pucks, right?*

Witty comebacks are the lifeblood of witty

banter, which is being able to take an element of what was said and attack it from a different angle without missing a beat. You should be able to see how this can play out. They are instant retorts that aren't hostile or combative, while addressing something gracefully. And this is a skill that you can use in many ways, as you are about to read in the next section.

Word of caution: Fight the temptation to rattle your comebacks off one after the other. Again, you have to remember that your goal is to get people to like you. You're not trying to prove a point or protect your pride.

You're just trying to keep your conversation from hitting awkward spots and dying a premature death. Firing off one comeback after another can kill whatever level of comfort you've managed to create because you will appear insecure, defensive, and full of bluster.

Instigate a Banter Chain

Have you ever noticed that some people seem to enjoy funny banter with everyone they meet?

It's not a coincidence. They are doing some of the exact things in this chapter to create that feeling whenever they want. It's easier than you think, but again, like most of the tactics here, you will be utilizing mental muscles that you haven't often practiced before.

There will be a slight learning curve, and you shouldn't expect to do it perfectly the first few times. That said, when you do grasp it more fully, you'll see the opportunities you've been missing to interact with people in certain ways. Also, the more you use this tactic, the better you'll get at it. Your initial attempts will likely fall flat, which can be embarrassing, but it's worth trying so that you can improve the next time.

One of the easy ways to inject humor in any

kind of conversation is when you instigate and create a banter chain. A banter chain involves both parties and allows a playful exchange that feels collaborative.

What's a banter chain? Well, it sounds something like this... and try to find the pattern that you were just using in the previous section of this chapter.

A: "That's a heck of a pant suit you've got there."

B: "Thanks, I had trouble finding a skirt to fit over my powerful thighs."

C: "You're squatting about 250 pounds now, right?"

D: "Closer to 350 pounds. Dogs are afraid of me when I walk by."

E: "You could use them as a screen for a drive-in movie theater."

F: "Did that last week. The double feature paid my rent this month. Did you know the *design for those two skyscrapers downtown was inspired by my legs?"*

That's a banter chain. You can see how the conversation flowed and how both parties played off each other. It was a collaborative effort and sounded like something you might find in a television show. In fact, that's what most of us think of when we think about witty banter: we're going with the flow and creating conversational chemistry.

But, what exactly just happened there, and how can you replicate it? Let's take a step back for a second.

A banter chain is notable because it's funny not based on what you say by itself, but how you play off the other person. If the other person catches on, then this gets funnier the farther along in the sequence you get. The situation gets more absurd, but that's the funny part.

It quickly becomes apparent to everyone listening that something funny is happening, and they will want to contribute to the shared experience. A joke was initiated, and both people **stayed in the joke** for as long as they could. Keep in mind that just as it's important to know how to instigate a banter chain, you must also end it and move on at an appropriate time before the chain feels overdone and the conversation becomes stale again.

When you say something and another person builds something on top of what you have said, you forge an instant bond. This creates an instant comfort amongst everybody participating. It's as if somebody is passing around a bottle and sharing a story. It feels good to everybody because they feel that they are part of something, and this can produce very funny situations.

If you have been to a comedy improv club, the banter chain might seem familiar. It is essentially improv comedy, where you collaborate with the other person to build a scene, or conversation in this case. Improv comedy and conversation really have the same overall goal (to play and amuse), so it's no surprise that the same techniques work for both.

If done properly, this chain of statements becomes weirder, funnier, and more outrageous. Everyone involved takes ownership over this, and all come away feeling like you've worked on something together. At the very least, you're going to have a solid inside joke to build upon for further interactions.

A banter chain has a few main elements and a few rules. Once you learn the mechanics, you're off to the races and can see how you prefer to approach it.

First, you need to misconstrue something in some way to enter the banter chain.

That's what statement B (*Thanks, I had trouble finding a skirt to fit over my powerful thighs.*) was. It doesn't matter how you misconstrue it, all you're doing is moving off-topic. You can also make an assumption about the other person out of nowhere, exaggerate something about their characteristics, or even make a non-sequitur. Alternatively, like in this case, you can make yourself the subject of banter. What's important is that it's a non-serious statement that the other person is aware is a joke.

You've initiated a joke (not *made* a joke), and it's an invitation for your conversational partner to join the banter on top of that joke. Remember, you always have the choice in how you want to reply and engage others.

Second, you have to see if the other person will play ball with you. When you make a non-serious statement, they'll either make a comment on it, or they will go back to the actual topic at hand. If they play ball, it looks like statement C (*You're squatting about 250 pounds now, right?*). If not, it would return to statement A (*That's a heck of a pant suit you've got there.*).

Third, if they play ball with you, congratulations! You're in a banter chain: they recognize what you're doing, they're playing along, and now you have to figure out how to play along back.

So, how do you do this? You build upon the direct response that they give you. You agree with them, and you add to it by *exaggerating and amplifying the sentiment*. That's what statement D (*Closer to 350 pounds. Dogs are afraid of me...*) does to statement C (*You're squatting about 250 pounds now, right?*), and so on. It takes the main sentiment of large thighs and makes the stakes bigger every time, playing with it in a creative manner.

The easiest way to continue the chain is to agree and amplify, which we learned earlier. You take what they say to be true, you agree, and then assume that the hyperbolic sentiment is true. If someone has big thighs, then to you, they have thighs that were the models for skyscrapers.

If they're still hanging with you, they'll do something similar and *stay in the joke*— that's the key here. You're staying in the joke that you've initiated, and prompted them to do the same.

You can continue this ad nauseam until someone breaks, but at that point, you've probably built an hour's worth of rapport.

The banter chain can be funny, but it depends on how it started and how it proceeds. Everyone involved makes the choice to either say "Haha, yeah," or actually participate in the chain.

Here is another example of a banter chain:

Normal statement: *"Hey, I like the coloring of that cat."*

Misconstrued statement to enter the banter chain: *"So, you think that cat is pretty sexy, huh?"*

Playing ball: *"Yeah, I want to ask it out on a date. You think I have a chance?"*

Hitting the ball back by agreeing and amplifying: *"Totally. Where will you take it? Somewhere fancy?"*

More banter: *"Italian. Some wine, some cheese, maybe some place with seafood. Let's see where the night takes us. Cats are nocturnal, after all."*

The great thing about the banter chain is that it allows you to make fun of each other and highlight a little bit of your wit and intelligence. It is consummate play. It is not just about exaggerating what the previous person said, since anybody can do that. What makes you a good participant in a banter chain is when you make a statement that is not only reasonable, but also funny because it is creative and creates references.

As another example, say you baked a friend some pastries which happened to be too sweet for your friend's liking. A banter chain in this situation might look something like this:

"How are the muffins?"

"They're very good. One bite is enough to

breed ants in my bloodstream."

"Oh great! At least now, when people point out how you're antsy all the time, you'll have actual ants to show for it."

"Yeah, that's why I eat your pastries at all. And I'm not too worried; they make good advancements in the research for diabetes treatment nowadays."

"Actually, those muffins were specifically ordered for mass production by those researchers to help them gain more test subjects. Talk about cooking for a cause."

Not only do you create a funny interaction, you are allowing each other to drop your guard. It creates a lighthearted moment. A bond is also created because you are collaborating with each other.

As amazing as this humor approach can be, you need to practice a little in advance to make sure you get it right. Practice exaggerating statements people say to you. How can you step it up in terms of absurdity and outlandishness? What are the extreme consequences of the people's statements? How many ways can you say that someone's thighs are huge without actually insulting them?

If someone makes a statement, what is the silly, hyperbolic consequence of taking that statement beyond its logical conclusion?

It's also helpful to realize that much of the time you will be making fun of yourself and exaggerating negatives about yourself in ridiculous ways. You have to let go of your ego. You might be insulted by things people say, but remember that banter is supposed to be lighthearted and fun. Allow yourself to be the target and exaggerate negatives about yourself. If it makes you feel better, you're going to be insulting yourself in absurd ways that can't possibly be true or hit *too* close to home.

With proper practice and the right approach, a banter chain can make a conversation last a long time, simply by agreeing and amplifying.

Go Beyond the Literal

If this chapter has one lesson so far, it's to stop taking every statement, question, or quip at face value. Stop taking them literally, and you'll find yourself in interesting conversation far more often. This means that you should be able to find multiple meanings behind a simple statement or question, but it requires going into a conversation with a completely different mindset.

It's a mindset of playing, exploration, and initiating jokes and humor. Most conversations you'll find yourself in on a daily basis are merely exchanges of information—these are face-value conversations that are mostly boring and don't build rapport very well.

I know this might still across as abstract, but here's what it looks like when someone is stuck in literal mode, and can't look beyond face value in a statement or question. Note that these are four separate examples, and the bolded statements are following the literal path.

"So I spent a fortune at the Apple store today."

"How much?"

"He plays guitar like a deity."

"What song did he play?"

"Last night's dinner made my taste buds cry."

"Where did you eat?"

"I quite enjoyed that speech."

"Me too, it was so informative."

These might seem like natural follow-up questions, and they are, but there are multiple ways of answering these remarks. The comments above happen to be ones that are very literal and taking the topic at face value. Again, that's going to strand you in boring small talk city.

When someone makes a statement like that, it's a subtle invitation to engage on something interesting, and it's also a sign that they don't necessarily want to talk about the literal topic itself. They want to talk about the emotions involved, and they are open to engaging in a joke on it. Once you've identified this emotion, make a remark that either misconstrues it to an absurd degree, or use a story that involves you and exaggerates that emotion. They've initiated a joke with you, and whether or not you take a literal stance on it, you do have the option to continue the joke.

When you stay literal, you miss opportunities for witty banter all day. People subconsciously initiate jokes with you, and you can initiate jokes with people in the same way. With some practice, you'll get better at not only recognizing good openings for banter, but creating ones out of seemingly ordinary statements.

How might we reply to those statements in a way that steps into a joke or humorous context? All you're doing is following the other person's lead and going with the flow.

"So I spent a fortune at the Apple store today."

"It's so expensive there I had to sell a kidney to buy my new phone."

"He plays guitar like a deity."

"More Buddha style, or would you say Ganesha style?"

"Last night's dinner made my taste buds cry."

"At least you didn't have to eat your own cooking. I made that mistake once."

"I quite enjoyed that speech." [Suppose that the speech's topic was horse breeding.]

"Me too, seems like the money is in horses, isn't it? What would we name our horse?"

So what did we do there to make those responses flow and become an entry to witty banter? We just gave responses that weren't literal, and that stayed 100 percent with the tone and flow of the statements made.

Our comments weren't forced and didn't appear like making a joke outright, and that's a small but important difference here. We took an invitation to a joke and initiated it, versus actually making a joke.

Jokes have strict structures—setup, context, punch line, and laughter. It's usually pretty obvious when someone is telling a joke, even in normal conversation. That means there's normally a specific time for you to laugh—which is hard to do if the joke isn't funny. Initiating and inviting someone to a joke doesn't create that problem.

All you have to do is practice thinking outside of the box. A key skill underlying this is the art of misconstruing.

The Art of Misconstruing

Some of the funniest situations I've seen in both movies and real life have come from simple misunderstandings.

Bob misunderstood what a proctologist did and scheduled four appointments, or Jenny misunderstood that the generic name for a painkiller is an analgesic, and is not pronounced nor administered the way she thought it was. Which one of those was from real life and which was from a movie? Well, both were from real life.

Those are instances of lightning caught in a bottle. Wouldn't it be great to create those moments when you want? You can take the lead instead of waiting for an opportunity to arise and essentially relying upon luck.

Misunderstanding and misinterpretation are great sources of humor because you play with two sets of expectations and operate in the gray area between them. Generally, the thing being misconstrued is fairly mundane, and the other person is most likely expecting a dry reply to their statement. Instead, what they're offered is something they hadn't considered, which piques their curiosity and makes them appreciate your wit.

Sometimes you have to be intentional about setting up these misunderstandings yourself, and that is the Art of Misconstruing: misunderstanding people in an intentional manner to bring about a comical situation.

In other words, playing dumb or confused and taking an entirely different meaning from what someone has said on purpose. It's one of the easiest and quickest ways to bring the conversation to a playful nature and break the mold of small talk.

Think of it as a transition from a boring topic into a more engaging conversation. Whatever perspective you take, it's simply a shift toward both parties enjoying themselves more.

The misconstruing tactic requires you to

stay in character for a split second while you do it. Strangely and counter-intuitively, this requires people to believe for a split second that you truly mean what you say. Otherwise, you convey mixed messages, and your words don't match up with the rest of your non-verbal or verbal delivery.

After that split second has passed, it will become obvious through your words and your delivery that you are making a joke. A wide, mischievous smile is the best giveaway for banter.

Here's a simplified example of misconstruing: when someone says "I like cats," you might reply with, "To EAT?" Pair your words with a shocked look on your face and eyes wide open. That's the character you are trying to convey.

You've misconstrued the other person by not picking up on their context or intent. Imagine how a foreigner might interpret those words because of a weak grasp of the English language. Where does the conversation go from there?

They'll likely join the banter with you and agree, such as "Yeah, but only stray cats. The domesticated ones are too fat."

Here's another example of how one of my friends used intentional misconstruing in a conversation. One time during a camping trip, I was amazed at a peculiar insect that had landed on my leg and I exclaimed, "What is this? I've never seen anything like this before." My friend leaned in closer to inspect what I was examining, then declared, "Yeah, that's a leg." My other friends who witnessed the scenario then also started examining their hands, arms, and feet while acting amazed as they uttered, "Ooh, what is this? I've never seen anything like this, have you?"

My friends misconstrued my fascination with the unique insect on purpose and reacted as if I had declared sudden astonishment of my true subject's backdrop, i.e. a boring, regular leg.

Misconstruing is one of the most common

ways of creating a humorous situation. It is the basis of many jokes because it's easy to take a situation and steer it in whatever direction you want. It allows you to initiate a joke with in most social situations.

It also helps you break out of typical, boring topics. By simply choosing to misconstrue, you can inject whatever perspective you want into a conversation at any point.

This technique is freeing and empowering! It doesn't get old and it can go a long way in adding life to otherwise generic or boring conversations.

What are some ways to misconstrue in a funny way?

Exaggerated Conclusion

This is where you misconstrue what someone says and take it to the extreme conclusion.

You exaggerate what they say to an exponential degree. If someone actually said X, you would pretend that they said X multiplied by one hundred and react accordingly.

For example, when someone says "I love my television," you might reply, "So do your parents know that you guys are living together before marriage?"

Instead of saying "I agree," or coming up with a statement in the same vein, or at the same intensity as the original statement, take the original statement, blow it out of proportion and put it in a different context.

If somebody says a politician has a good point, a really funny exaggeration would be "Yes, he is the epitome of this country's political evolution, let's use him for breeding." Notice that the way this statement is delivered will make a huge difference to the way it's received. Even a minimally mocking tone makes this line appear like an overly extreme reaction. But a playful demeanor will earn you a much more positive response. Though it might be tempting to stay away from jokes about controversial topics like politics, they are often the ones that have the most impact.

To summarize, misconstruing is all about blowing up somebody's statement to an absurd and exaggerated form.

Here are some more examples:

Say someone comments, "That coffee was terrible!" You could reply, "I agree, my car's battery water is tastier."

When somebody laments, "My handwriting is horrible," you can poke fun on the person by responding "Yes, deciphering hieroglyphs would be an easier task than trying to make out your script."

In reply to the line, "I'll call you when I get home," you can say, "I didn't know it's possible to make a phone call from Mars, but okay."

What makes this form of misconstruing powerful is the absurdity of your exaggeration. It should be so absurd that it is no longer believable. That's where the humor comes from. A lot of people screw up this technique when they don't exaggerate enough. They fall somewhere in between the truly funny exaggerated form and the generic statement.

Say someone declares, "I'm so hungry, I'm for sure gonna eat a lot in this meal." If you reply with "Yeah, it's no doubt you can finish off this whole pie by yourself once you get to it. Don't worry, the rest of us can find something else to eat," you're not exaggerating enough to make your quip hilarious. What's worse, if that person is *actually* able to eat the pie by themselves, then you will have created an awkward situation likely to make the other party feel conscious about how much they actually eat.

Here's another bad example. Imagine someone comments, "I haven't had time to shop for new clothes recently." If you respond by saying, "Oh, that's why you've been dressing so shabbily lately," that person is not likely to take your criticism as good-natured ribbing, even if that was your original intention. The problem here is that you haven't exaggerated your response enough to make it obvious you're both supposed to be laughing, and not that you're the only one laughing at them.

Instead of packing in a punch, the above replies fall flat and are likely to elicit raised eyebrows at best or insulted feelings at worst. So if you want to use this technique, make sure you really blow it up and make it out of this world. That way, it's obvious to the other person that you are making fun and they can laugh along.

Imagine if for the above bad scenarios, you would instead respond with, "Yes, I know it was really you who finished off the gingerbread house in Hansel and Gretel" and "Oh, that's why you've been looking like a homeless person these days." Those sound easier to laugh to with the other person, don't they? Nevertheless, remember to refrain from picking things to exaggerate that the other person might genuinely care about.

Playful Tease

This is when you misconstrue what a person says to be negative about themselves. Assume that they are making a self-deprecating statement and agree with them.

For example, when someone says, "I love watching television" you might say, "Yes, but you know that television doesn't replace friends, right?"

What did we do here? We assumed that they were lamenting the fact that they loved television and had no one to spend time with, so television was their only choice.

Misconstrue that they are being negative, and you are just agreeing with them.

If someone was to say, "I love this shirt," you might reply, "Don't worry, we'll go shopping for a shirt that *actually* looks good." You take the person's judgment and redirect it against them. With the right facial expressions, this statement will not come off as an attack. Instead, this will land as a nice joke.

Another example would be if somebody notes, "The burgers taste terrific here." You might respond, "I guess it's understandable that you've ruined your taste buds having nothing but cold cereal for breakfast for years."

Finally, if someone was to say, "She's my favorite singer," you might reply, "We'll work on your taste."

Again, watch your facial expression. There is a thin line between teasing and downright insulting somebody. Make sure that all the other signals you send out from your body language, tone of voice, eye contact, and facial expressions convey the fact that you are just joking.

It goes without saying, but you need to be careful about this around sensitive people. Some people, no matter what you say, will take your words offensively and won't be able to take a playful rib. It's probably best to not use this tactic until you know people a little bit better, and definitely not about something you think they might be insecure about.

If you feel that you may have unintentionally offended someone, you can quickly follow up your playful tease with a compliment about the same thing that you teased them about. To take the shirt example, if you say "we'll go shopping for a shirt that actually looks good" and the other person seems put off by your remark, you can cover up your mistake by saying, "Just kidding, I actually need shirts that look as good for myself. Still up for that shopping trip?" Not only have you explicitly pointed out that you were joking, but also reversed the situation by making a joke at your own expense.

The other way of using the playful tease is to assume that *they* are insulting and being negative about you. Then you just react to that and act as if you are defending yourself.

Let's take the examples above, "She's my favorite singer" and "I love this shirt." Misconstruing as if *they* are teasing *you* sounds like, "I know, my ears don't work because she's not my favorite," and, "So you're saying I could never pull that shirt off?"

If all else fails, you can just act shocked by the words and make a big deal out of them even though the person said something unremarkable. For example, when someone says "I love watching television," then you say, "Oh my gosh, television?!"

Another example is when someone says "That shirt is terrible," you say, "Terrible?! Are you crazy?!"

The bottom line is that misconstruing subverts people's expectations. It breaks the pattern of the conversation and spices it up. If done properly, you shake people out of the generic pattern of the conversation and highlight your sense of humor. Focus on your demeanor, delivery, and expressions to have the maximum effect.

And as you can see, it's quite easy to jump in and out of conversation topics while using this technique.

Takeaways

- This chapter will teach you how to be a witty comeback machine. If you're the kind of person who thinks of smart replies twenty minutes after a conversation ends, the techniques laid out here will help you come up with them much quicker. It's a matter of thinking non-literally, non-conventionally, and non-linearly, and realizing that a conversation is an opportunity for play rather than information dissemination.
- If someone is teasing you, there are two methods you can use which will help you come up with a witty comeback. You can either take the thing they're teasing you about and exaggerate it to the point of absurdity, or point out a funny, but positive side effect of that thing

you're being teased about.

- While delivering comebacks, it's important to use the right tone and act like you can take a joke. Nobody likes a bad sport, and you'll want to indicate that you're joking through your demeanor and expressions. Smile wryly after saying your comeback, and use a tone that conveys indifference rather than annoyance.

- Our next few tricks rely on the art of misconstruing. The banter chain is the first of these. Banter chains are a series of exchanges that rely on you having misconstrued an ordinary remark as the other person plays along. You put forth a purposeful misinterpretation, and if they bite on it, you have now entered what you can call a banter chain, and can continue to ramp it up.

- Another technique relying on misconstruing is the exaggerated conclusion. Here, you basically take a statement and exaggerate it exponentially to step out of the ordinary and into something that can resemble play. Our last misconstruing trick is the playful tease, where you give your conversation partner a bit of good-natured ribbing that leaves you both laughing.

Chapter 4. Funny on Command

If there's a theme I would hope you've learned thus far from this book, it's that to be funny, you don't always need to actively attempt to be entertaining or tell jokes like a stand-up comedian.

If you constantly try to crack jokes, make connections, and set up punch lines, chances are that you're probably going to be more obnoxious than amusing. As we've seen from previous chapters, not all wittiness and humor is like that. Much of what makes remarks funny and witty is the fact that they're unexpected. However, if you're constantly spewing them out, things can become predictable, and even annoying because your behavior lends the impression that you're trying too hard.

This book is focused on making your personality wittier naturally. Think of someone who happens to have flaming red shoes and whose favorite shirt has cartoon zebras fighting. He's not trying to be funny, he just has a disposition and approach to life that might be more conducive to being naturally humorous. He would describe a pie in terms of deliciousness versus flavor.

Vivid Imagery

To be funny, you don't have to intentionally try. You can use vivid and outlandish imagery to describe what you see and make analogies.

You're reading this book in English, and in the English language, there are words that are superior to others for comic effect. You could say that someone is "funny," but you could also say that they "made your cheeks ache from laughing."

We use lazy, uninspired language on a daily basis, and part of being funnier is to slowly replace those common terms and phrases with more flavorful ones. You could call someone "stupid," but you could also call them a "buffoon" or "nincompoop"—objectively rarer and sillier words, and less directly insulting than "stupid."

Other examples of words that are inherently funny, or at least unusual, are:

- Lake Titicaca (a real lake)
- Dingleberry
- Discombobulate
- Blubber
- Poppycock
- Gobbledygook

Not that you should be using those words specifically, but there is definitely a range of more creative words you can add to your everyday language. The first step here is to realize that we naturally speak in a boring and overly sanitized manner. Alternatives like the ones listed don't just sound funnier, they fill our minds with funny images and thoughts of berries, lakes, etc., that are completely unrelated to the context the word is being used in.

Our vocabulary and daily sense of imagery is sorely lacking, and we need to fix that to become more interesting and funny without visible effort. Remember in your English (or SAT) classes when you learned new vocabulary words—the ones with four or five syllables?

You'd pepper them into your vocabulary subtly to make yourself sound intelligent and erudite. See? I just did it myself.

If you commit to replacing parts of your vocabulary, and thinking for a split second more when you describe things, these small changes can make a big difference as to how you are perceived. Someone who "dances funny" is barely a blip on our screen, but someone who "dances like a gorilla cooking an omelet" catches our attention immediately.

Usage #1

The first step is to destroy normal adjectives from your vocabulary and replace them with something that you have to think about. Other people often will not have actively thought about your examples, and the result will be unexpected.

If you wanted to say that your weekend was "good," what might be better and more descriptive ways of doing that?

Good -> imaginative -> splendid -> like a big Bloody Mary -> better than using the bathroom after a long car ride -> almost as good as Christmas morning.

If you wanted to say that you love coffee, what might be a better and more descriptive way of doing that?

I love coffee -> it is my lifeblood -> I'm dead without it -> my blood is fifty percent caffeine -> I would bathe in it if I could -> I drink so much my urine looks like coffee too.

See the difference?

It's not difficult, but it's not easy to come up with on the fly, either. This is a mindset you have to proactively cultivate. Whenever you come across a normal adjective, think of what other synonyms you might use in giving people descriptive answers.

When you use better words and phrases, you'll make people react to them because you are saying much more than just the words and phrases themselves. If you struggle to come up with good alternatives, you can always fall back on using analogies. Like in the first example involving "good," you can use "as good as...," ideally with a comparison that invokes common imagery.

As another example, if you had to think of an alternative for "bad," you could use "as bad as the seventh circle of hell."

Usage #2

Another way to inject vivid and outlandish imagery into your daily speaking is to simply choose to describe observations, actions, and objects in an unconventional and creative way.

For example, comedienne Amy Schumer has a great example of this when she describes her sleeping positions. She *could* describe how she sleeps as "messy" or "weird." She could even go another level up and say she sleeps like an "unsalted pretzel."

The unsalted pretzel gives you a mental image, but she does even better.

She describes her sleeping position to be "as if she fell from the top of a building" or "in the shape of a swastika."

There's your instant mental image, which now has the added intelligent humor of combining two very different concepts (sleep and swastika, sleep and falling off of a building).

Another example of this is from PJ O'Rourke, who described his experiences with local military in the Philippines, involving contact with a small policeman who amazed him.

He described the policeman as very intimidating and scary, but also very petite. His exact phrasing was, "He looked like an attack hamster."

Even if you're not trying to be funny, just the way you come up with analogies on contrast and compare different concepts can make for really amusing descriptions.

How do you master the art of humorous descriptions?

The first step is to attempt to disassociate from the meaning of what you see, and just focus on the elements and traits of what's in front of you.

For example, in the case of PJ O'Rourke, you would disassociate that you were looking at a police officer, and focus on the elements and traits of the police officer.

He was small, petite, scary, intimidating, powerful, fierce, authoritative, serious, severe, and elfin.

What are two distinct concepts that would fit the descriptions above?

O'Rourke identified a small animal, a hamster, and also played on the fact that this person had a strong physical and military capability who can attack. When you put those two concepts together you may come up with the funny image of an attack hamster.

This type of humor really stretches your imagination and creativity. You're forced to brainstorm what the basic elements are related to, and what they resemble on a physical level. These weird combinations create funny images like Amy Schumer's description of sleeping.

Another example is when a character in the *Avengers: Endgame* movie told the flabbier-than-before Thor, "You look like melted ice cream." The mental imagery such choice of words evokes is instantly striking and funny, and it derives much of its humor from the easily recognizable resemblance of "melted ice cream" with Thor's silhouette. It's worth noting that you may want to be careful about using this technique to comment on people's weight in casual conversations, of course. Keep in mind that sensitivity as to what would come across as insulting more than amusing still holds prime importance in social situations.

How might using imagery be applied in your daily conversations? Say somebody asked how you are after a particularly punishing trekking experience. You may go with the usual "I'm so tired," or you may spruce up your response by instead saying, "My feet are lumps of custard and my knees feel like unoiled, creaky door hinges." If you want to tell someone "It was so hot yesterday," you could instead opt for the more stimulating line, "Yesterday, the Earth moved to take Mercury's place beside the sun." The vivid images these statements create in your listener's mind will surely keep humdrum chats at bay.

Another great benefit about this particular approach to humor is that it necessarily increases your vocabulary. It also exercises your creative thinking in coming up with weird analogies and weird connections on the fly. Compare this with simply saying the same words over and over again like "good" and "bad," which leaves you coming off as an unimaginative and fairly dull.

Usage #3

The final way, and a more hit-or-miss way, to use better imagery is to use popular culture references to replace adjectives. The more widely known the reference is, the better the joke.

However, some people will completely miss the reference and not know what you're talking about. That's why this can be hit-or-miss.

This is very simple. Let's pick a well-known reference to use: the corruption of the Olympic Games. It's not something that people know details about, but it's something that people generally know exists. See—it's tough.

What traits would you assign to this reference? Corruption, unfairness, inequality, deviousness, sneakiness, and so on.

You can use the traits of the reference to describe things, such as "That cashier gave me a one-dollar bill back instead of a ten-dollar bill. Does he work for the Olympics or something?"

You're replacing the word "corrupt" with a popular culture reference—a much more descriptive, timely, and vivid way of speaking.

Let's use another well-known reference: the television show *Game of Thrones.*

Use the traits of the television show to describe something—in this example, "addicting": "This octopus pie is almost as addicting as watching *Game of Thrones*. It's amazing."

The key is to get people to visualize the references and laugh from the disconnect.

With that said, make sure the references you use are appropriate. It pays to devote some attention to the ages and contexts of the people you're speaking to. For example, a third extremely common pop culture reference that is often used humorously is "that's what she said!" from *The Office*. Though it's a great way to make sexual puns out of random statements among friends, a more formal setting might make it appear distasteful.

You may also use references to describe people in your social circle in a more interesting way. Rather than saying that your little nephew is resourceful, you might instead say, "The way he puts together his own toys will put MacGyver to shame!" Of course, note that anyone born later than the '90s might not get this reference so well. This is where your insight on generational differences comes in—try to match your references with the age of the person you're talking with. That way, you heighten the chances that your reference will be a hit rather than a miss.

It only takes a little bit of effort to begin replacing the words and phrases in your vocabulary to sound like a completely new person. Unfortunately, we only get one chance to make first impressions on people, so make them count! If you watch any relatively popular movies or TV shows, you can also use references from them since there is a greater likelihood that someone else would've heard of it. With some luck, not only will you come across as funny, but if the other person is a fellow fan, you'll also have something to bond over.

The Comic Triple

The comic triple is one of the easiest and most recognizable jokes in the world.

You may not realize it, but you've heard the comic triple many, many times in your life.

It's about time to learn how to use it effectively!

Before we dive into the mechanics and steps, here's a quick example of the comic triple.

You know what my favorite part about coffee is? The energy boost, the aroma, and the yellowing effect on your teeth.

The comic triple draws its power from the fact that people have been conditioned in many ways to process information and take significance in groups of threes.

Think about where this pattern of threes exists in our lives. It's everywhere.

The Three Little Pigs. Newton's three laws of physics. Goldilocks and the Three Bears. The three parts of a joke. The three phases of a story. Destiny's Child. *Charlie's Angels.* Kirk, Spock and Dr. McCoy. The Three Stooges. The Holy Trinity.

There is something about the number three

and how the brain organizes itself.

Once you start looking, you'll see it everywhere. For good reason, it's also the method management experts use to most effectively teach and disseminate information. For example, notable leadership expert Kevin Kruse is known for only giving people three pieces of information at a time. This way, people can maintain their focus and not get distracted. Some argue that if you can't boil something down to three main points, it's not an inherently sound argument.

You can even put it this way: the human brain is certainly capable of retaining more, but for greatest impact, comedic or not, three works best.

That is the background for why this technique is indeed the comic *triple*.

When you make a list of three things, you generally make a list of three similar things. They might even be synonyms. For example, you might describe a woman as sexy, cute, and beautiful, or a new type of car as exciting, cool, and innovative.

When you make any type of list, you build an expectation that you'll be enhancing the sentiment, and using the list to emphasize one point overall. People expect only one direct line of thinking.

The comic triple surprises people because where they might expect a list to contain only one sentiment, the comic triple contains two, and the two sentiments couldn't be more different.

The first two elements are something expected and in line with each other. They are relevant to each other and flow naturally; the third is what springs the surprise on the listener. The tension of the buildup is released, and the surprise makes people laugh. Again, what makes this work is the surprising and unexpected nature of the third element.

Let's bring this out of the abstract and into the concrete for a moment: the first two elements will be positive, and the last element will be negative, or vice versa. Now we can continue with less confusion.

One famous example of the comic triple is from Mark Twain, made in reference to government data and how to analyze it: "There are lies, damned lies, and statistics."

Everyone hates being lied to. We are outraged when people in government, or those taking advantage of the government's influence, lie to benefit themselves. We're so outraged that we go along with the "damned lies" part because it's more of the same insidious manipulation of the public. We're enraged. We expect the last part of this list to build to the epiphany of corruption with something like, "The lies that make you unable to sleep at night."

That's the logical conclusion, right?

Instead, we're thrown for a complete loop when Twain mentions statistics. Statistics are the opposite of lying, assuming they are not being manipulated or faked. People instinctively trust statistics. Therefore, this is the exact opposite sentiment of the first two elements of Twain's triple.

Here's another example of a comic triple from comedian Chris Rock: "There are only three things women need in life: food, water, and compliments."

That quote is funny because food and water go together. The sentiment is simply based on sustenance and basic human needs. Usually, when people say you only need three things to survive, the third element people are probably anticipating is air or shelter.

Chris Rock dashes your sense of anticipation and expectation by completing the triple with "compliments," which is a small jab at women, as well as the opposite sentiment of a basic human need.

In the TV show *The Big Bang Theory*, the character Sheldon Cooper also delivered a comic triple while he chewed on a lamb kebab: "And what a civilization is the

Greeks'...They gave us science, democracy...and little cubes of charred meat that taste like sweat!"

The first two Greek contributions he mentioned, science and democracy, are both positive. He then followed up with a negative comment on Greek food, which cued a holler from the audience as it was an unexpected twist from the positive line of thought.

Here is another example from comedian Jon Stewart, former host of *The Daily Show*: "I celebrated Thanksgiving in an old-fashioned way. I invited everyone in the neighborhood to my house, we had an enormous feast, and then I killed them and took their land."

Two positives and one negative. Are we seeing the pattern yet?

Jon Stewart is making fun of the history of Native Americans and European settlers in the United States. When the first English settlers came to New England they had such a tough time that they almost starved to death. It was only when Native Americans showed them how to pick the right berries, prepare the right food, and otherwise survive in that new environment that they were able to raise enough food and the colony survived.

To commemorate that, the United States has celebrated Thanksgiving in some form or another since 1863. Stewart pokes fun at that traditional Thanksgiving in the historical context and also reminds people of the violence against indigenous people that went with the colonization of the United States. Two positives and one negative.

How do you make the comic triple work for you?

Step one: think of your topic or theme.

This can be pretty much anything that has two contrasting features. Most things have at least one positive quality, and one that is either negative or can be exaggerated in a way that makes for a good contrast with the positive quality. As we've seen, it can be different foods, genders, occasions, etc. For this example, we'll use the theme of coffee.

Step two: list two positives, or list two negatives.

List two things that are related to coffee in positive or negative ways.

For example, being energetic, waking up, having a routine, the aroma; these are generally positive descriptors that you might think about when you think of coffee. Keep in mind that these are things that everyone agrees are good about coffee. Not everyone might agree that taste is a positive descriptor for coffee, but aroma and energy are traits most will agree with.

Step three: list one negative, or one positive.

You go the opposite route, the opposite sentiment as what you used in step two.

So what's negative about coffee? This sets up the contrast. Stained teeth, being over-caffeinated, drug cartels, addiction, and spilling it on white clothing.

Step four: put it all together.

"I have coffee every morning. I love the aroma, how it wakes me up, and how I always seem to spill it on my white shirts."

Do you see how the anticipation and expectation builds through the first two elements, and then is completely reversed in the last element?

Here's another example now that we've gone through the process once. This time, we'll deconstruct a completed comic triple: "I love everything about her. Her smile, her sense of style, and how she never has any clue where she wants to go for dinner."

You take a person, and start with two positives, then you reverse the emotion and go negative.

Don't expect to hit a home run the first time you step up to the plate with this comedic approach. It can be mastered after a bit of practice. Keep it simple, and try to think in black and white and negative and positive terms.

Once you get good at the comic triple, you'll be able to assemble it on the fly. That's one of the best parts—you can list two positive aspects while brainstorming for the third, negative aspect, all spontaneously.

Misdirection Aplenty

Misdirection is when you say one thing and then proceed with an immediate opposite. For example, "It's a secret, but let me tell you immediately," or, "That show is great, except for everyone in it."

It seems confusing, but what you are doing is breaking a sentence into two parts.

You're stating something in the first part, then contradicting it immediately in the second. People won't immediately be sure of what you mean, and part of the humor comes from this introduced confusion. You have both positive and negative, or vice versa, in the same sentence.

The second part of the sentence is the element that people will react to, while the first part is typically the setup. The second is your true sentiment on the topic.

This formula is the secret to the humor in such lines as George Jessel's "The human brain is a wonderful organ. It starts to work as soon as you are born and doesn't stop until you get up to deliver a speech." Douglas Adams also used it when he said, "I love deadlines. I like the whooshing sound they make as they fly by." Here's another example: "I love dogs, but I hate seeing, hearing, and touching them," or, "This juice is awesome. Did it come from the garbage disposal?"

Why does misdirection work?

Most of us try to be polite to people. We use euphemisms frequently, and we don't say what we really feel. The first part of a misdirecting statement is what people expect—politeness. Then, you contradict yourself and give them a dose of reality, which sets up a humorous contrast since you have deviated from what most people expect and would say themselves. As you might have observed, ironic similes also make use of misdirection to derive comedic effect.

Last but not least, misdirection is a funny way to express your feelings on something. If you really feel X about a topic, then use misdirection! "Opposite of X, but actually X," will almost always be received far better than "Gosh, I hate X."

Sarcasm is a way for people to say things without saying them, and is the most common way we use misdirection.

Think about how Chandler Bing from the television show *Friends* talks. If he says something is wonderful, he says *it's wonnnnderful* in a tone that immediately lets you know that he thinks the opposite.

Sarcasm functions like a social cue—both are ways to express something without having to explicitly say it. In that way, it's a great device for handling uncomfortable topics or pointing out the elephant in the room without directly offending people (or pointing). It allows us to walk a tightrope, as long as we don't fall into the pit of passive-aggressiveness.

At some level, most of us can appreciate sarcasm because we know what is being accomplished. It can even be the basis for your own personal brand of humor. Standup comics often use it to great effect.

Chances are, you are already using sarcasm regularly without being fully aware of it. Sarcasm is mostly used as friendly banter with a friend or acquaintance with whom you are comfortable saying something negative. For example, consider that you've committed a minor gaffe at work, for example forgetting to return a borrowed file before it's due. If a close colleague teases you about it, you may reply with a sarcastic, "Oh yes, this is scandalous! This would for sure be in the headlines tomorrow!" But if it's your strict boss who sternly calls you out on it, you would not be likely to make a sarcastic announcement in response.

Sarcasm is usually used to poke fun at someone or something, and is heavily context and audience-dependent. If you are around somebody who enjoys wit and has a sarcastic sense of humor, it will be quite welcome.

But around others who don't share the same sense of humor, are less secure, or don't like you, it's too easy for them to interpret your attempts at sarcastic humor as a full-fledged insult. They might just think that you are an insulting jackass. That's not what you're aiming for here.

Using it in the wrong context will cause people to think you lack empathy or, worse, get your jollies from hurting other people's feelings. There will be others who simply won't get the sarcasm, no matter how obvious you make it. They won't be insulted, just very confused. You'll want to avoid both outcomes.

However, choose the correct context and sarcasm can make you more likeable and charming. It also makes you look intelligent and witty. In some social circles, appropriate levels of sarcasm are not only welcomed, but required.

Now that you have a clearer idea about the proper context of sarcasm, the next step is to articulate the elements to make sure you don't just insult people left and right in your attempts at building rapport. If your annoying coworker understood sarcasm better, they might be as funny as they think they are.

For the most part, **sarcasm is saying the *opposite* of (1) an objective fact, (2) a subjective emotion, or (3) thought.**

It makes a contradictory statement about a situation to either emphasize or downplay its effect.

Objective fact: Bob plays Tetris at work constantly.

Sarcastic statement: *Bob, you are the busiest man I know.*

Subjective emotion or thought: It is hilarious that Bob plays Tetris at work constantly.

Sarcastic statement: *Bob deserves a medal for worker of the year.*

Here's another one.

Objective fact: There is a surprising amount of traffic lately.

Sarcastic statement: *What are we going to do when we get to our destination super early?*

Subjective emotion or thought: I hate traffic so much.

Sarcastic statement: *This traffic is the best part of my day.*

That's the first and most common use of sarcasm. Now let's lay out a framework for different types of sarcasm and exactly when and how you can use it. You'll be surprised how formulaic and methodical you can get with this, and subsequently with humor.

When someone says or does something very obvious, you respond by saying something equally obvious.

Bob: "That road is very long."

You: "You are very observant."

Bob: "It's so hot today!"

You: "I see you're a meteorologist in training."

Poor Bob: "This menu is huge!"

You: "Glad to see you've learned to read!"

The next application of sarcasm is when something bad happens. You say something about how that good or bad event reflects on the other person.

If it's good, you say that it reflects badly on them; if it's bad, you say it reflects well on them.

Bob: "I dropped my coffee mug."

You: "You've always been so graceful."

Bob: "I got an F on my math test."

You: "Now I know who to call when my calculator breaks."

You observe Poor Bob dropping a cup of coffee and state "You would make a great baseball catcher. Great hands!"

Proper delivery is crucial for sarcasm. This can mean the difference between people laughing at your sarcastic joke, or thinking that you're serious in your sentiment and branding you an overall jerk. Also keep in mind that sarcasm is perhaps the most overused technique to create humor. Use it sparingly, but effectively.

You have to make it clear that you're being sarcastic and give others a sign indicating so. Otherwise, people will feel uncomfortable at the uncertainty. Are you just being mean, or are you trying to be funny?

The most common way to do this is with a combination of a deadpan vocal tone and a wry smile or smirk. With deadpan delivery, you don't laugh while you're saying it; you appear completely serious. Then, you break into a smile to alleviate the tension and clue others in to your true intention.

Now that you know when to deliver sarcastic remarks, it's also important to learn about how to receive them and be a good audience. Let's pretend that you are Poor Bob from earlier, and insert a reply for him.

Bob: "That road is very long."

You: "You are very observant."

Bob: "You know it. I'm like an eagle."

Bob: "It's so hot today!"

You: "I see you're a meteorologist in training."

Bob: "I can feel it in my bones. It's my destiny."

Poor Bob: "This menu is huge!"

You: "Glad to see you've learned to read!"

Redeemed Bob: **"I can also count to ten**."

You need to amplify their statement and what they are implying. Does this look familiar? It's a self-deprecating remark + a witty comeback!

When you respond to sarcasm this way, it creates a greater bond. Everybody is comfortable, and you create a funny situation and potential for greater banter.

And just as important, you don't come off as a bad sport or someone who can't take a joke.

However, there is a downside when dealing with sarcasm. A lot of people who rely on sarcastic humor, pretty much on an automatic basis, are actually masking passive-aggressive personalities. They're constantly using sarcasm as a defense mechanism to hide their true feelings. They use sarcasm to pass off their otherwise negative emotions. They might be doing this to you, so it's important to know how to sidestep their subconsciously vicious attacks.

In such cases, responding with sarcasm will only encourage them. It indicates that misusing sarcasm in that way is acceptable. If you find someone being overly sarcastic with you in ways that are passive-aggressive, approach them and politely convey that their sarcasm feels hostile, even if they didn't intend it to be so.

Next, we have irony. Irony is a type of humor that is very close to sarcasm, and often confused with it.

Here's the official definition from Dictionary.com, just because it's something that people can struggle with nailing down: "the expression of one's meaning by using language that normally signifies the opposite, typically for humorous or emphatic effect."

This is different from sarcasm in a few ways. First, irony is generally about situations and incidents, not about people. Something happens which is the opposite of what you expected. When you're presented with an irony, like a fire station burning down, it will quite obviously be ironic, and not sarcastic. However, sarcasm is usually more derogatory in nature. You're saying things you don't mean. The definition of sarcasm is "the use of irony to mock or convey contempt." Thus, you can see how saying "You are very observant" when someone says "This road is very long" is sarcasm, not irony, because of the element of mockery inherent in the former remark.

Ironic humor is when something that is the exact opposite of what you might expect occurs. Another way to define irony is when you say something, but mean the exact opposite of what you expect.

In other words, the words that come from your mouth are the opposite of the emotion you are feeling. If you're starving, an ironic statement might be something like, "I'm so full I need to unbuckle my belt. It's like Thanksgiving in July."

Ironic humor draws its power from contrasts. There is a contrast between literal truth and perceived truth. In many cases, ironic humor stems from frustration or disappointment with our ideals. The way we imagine the world should be produces comedy when it clashes with how the world actually is.

Ironic humor is usually used to make a funny point about something or to point something out. For example, when you see a bird landing on a sign that says "No birds allowed," that's ironic humor. The sign bans birds, but the bird is there sitting on the sign. The expectation that the sign ensures there will be no birds in the vicinity failed.

Another example is when you see a car with a logo on the door saying "Municipal Traffic Reduction Committee," and the car, along with everybody else, is stuck in two hours of bumper to bumper traffic. There is a profound ironic comedy there, as you would expect the traffic management planning committee would do a better job so they wouldn't be stuck in traffic themselves.

Irony is all about finding contrast and drawing some interesting and creative judgment out of it. As the examples indicate, ironic humor is more a matter of observation than one of spontaneity or creativity. You're more likely to find and point out things that are ironic than come up with something that is.

Ironic humor, on the other hand, is when you intentionally imply the opposite meaning of what you say. When we think about how to use irony conversationally, what we're really asking is what ways can we convey two messages at one time?

Words Versus Tone

Remember, irony is more about observing contrasts. As a point of distinction, if you observe this, it's likely to be irony, but if you use it, it's more likely to sarcasm.

"I'M A PEOPLE PERSON! PEOPLE LIKE ME!"

"I am very happy right now. I am ecstatic," said in a very grumpy and exasperated voice.

"I'm going to kill you. You are so annoying," said with a saccharine and overly sweet tone.

You can go both ways on this: positive

words with negative tone, or negative words with positive tone. You know you've done it correctly if it's apparent to the other person what you're trying to say. If you cause confusion when you try this method, it means that the tone of your voice isn't obvious enough.

Words Versus Body Language

This is where you use your words to say one thing, but your body language, facial expressions, and other non-verbal cues scream something different. Imagine the same examples from the previous variation, but instead of your vocal tone, your body language and facial expressions are the opposite of your words.

"I'M A PEOPLE PERSON! PEOPLE LIKE ME!" would be said with a huge scowl, and making a knife motion across your neck to indicate that you hate people.

"I am very happy right now. I'm ecstatic," would be said while shaking your head, gesturing that you want to jump off a bridge, all with a disgusted face.

"I'm going to kill you. You're so annoying," would be said while smiling angelically, attempting to hug the other person gently, and stroking their shoulder as if to calm them down.

Ironic humor uses different elements that clash with each other to produce contrast in the mind of your audience. It creates a sense of the unexpected and excites the people you are speaking with. Its reason for being funny operates in a similar way to misconstruing. It is all about the contrast and creating an unexpected moment.

You can go both ways on this variation as well. You can pair positive words with negative non-verbal expression, or negative words with positive non-verbal expression. Of course, you can combine your non-verbals (body language and facial expressions), tone of voice, and actual words for greatest effect.

Ironic Simile

A simile is a literary device where you say one thing is like another thing. At least, that's a normal simile. Some examples include "as smooth as velvet," "as clean as a whistle," and "as brave as a lion."

An *ironic simile* is a comparison between two things that are not similar at all, except for one shared trait or descriptor.

To create an ironic simile, first make a statement that is the opposite of how you actually feel, and then compare it to a situation that is also the opposite of how you feel. Explaining an ironic simile is like trying to explain what a color looks like, so here are a few examples.

"I'm as likely to vote for that candidate as I would set up an appointment with a proctologist with uncontrollable muscle spasms."

You say that you would vote for the candidate, but then you introduce something that is supremely negative.

That's ironic simile—a comparison to something that is the opposite of what you mean. Notice that the sentence typically starts with a deceptive description such as, "likely to vote for that candidate." Then, the latter part of that statement does a backpedal on its initial message by introducing a comparison that would evoke an opposite sentiment, i.e. "set up an appointment with a proctologist with uncontrollable muscle spasms." The end result is a declaration of just how *unlikely* you are to vote for that candidate, the complete opposite of the initial impression the sentence made.

Let's take another example:
"I'm as sad as a dog with a bone."

In terms of the formula we reviewed above, the deceptive introduction is "as sad as," then the backpedal happens when you say "a dog with a bone." Usually when a dog has bone in his mouth, the last emotion you would describe is sadness, as dogs with bones are quite happy. Thus, such an ironic simile has you ending up with an expression of utter happiness regardless of your initially mentioned descriptor, "sad."

Now how about the following example? "That person is as flexible as a brick."

The humor here is that you highlight the fact that this person is not flexible at all. The ironic simile works by first deceptively describing the person as "flexible," but then backpedaling on it by comparing his flexibility to a brick. Unless you are dealing with a brick made of super-conducting jelly, chances are, the brick in question is extremely inflexible and rigid.

Here are a few more examples of ironic simile:

"Our teacher's discussion of Heisenberg's principle was as clear as mud."

"She has all the social graces of a steamroller."

"Being the third wheel on their date was as enjoyable as a root canal."

Can you create some ironic similes yourself too? Practice putting together your own every time you want to describe an experience or a memorable feeling. This way, coming up with amusing ironic similes in casual conversations will be about as difficult as counting to ten.

Hyperbole

This is when you say something negative about a positive statement, or you say something positive about a negative statement—in a hyperbolic and exaggerated way.

"Flat tire? Best news of the week."

Negative occurrence, then positive statement.

Usually when people say something to this effect, they draw your attention to how negative or positive something actually was. Now that they got a flat tire, they have a new worry on top of the previous minor irritations and annoyances this week has delivered.

"It's not a problem, I'll probably run four miles later. It's only my injured ankle and foot!"

This is hilarious precisely because you are making light of the fact that you have a serious medical condition.

Irony is funny, but you shouldn't overuse it, otherwise people won't know what you're saying, and people might not take you seriously at all. You're conveying a mixed message intentionally, so at some point people have to get to know your baseline personality and set of reactions.

Yet another way to use misdirection to your advantage is to answer questions in the opposite. If someone expects you to say yes, say no, and vice versa. The more obvious the better. Like so many tricks we've covered before, this one also relies on the element of surprise that comes with an unexpected answer.

Jennifer Lawrence uses this one fairly often. When she was on Ellen Degeneres' show after rising to fame thanks to *Hunger Games*, she was asked whether she'd gotten used to all the fame and attention that came with being a celebrity. Since she was only around twenty at the time, most would've expected a clear "No" from her. Instead, she went the other way and said "Yes!" Her demeanor made it apparent that she hadn't actually gotten used to it, essentially turning her remark into a sarcastic one.

To generate the most laughter, use this technique only in the case of yes/no questions where the other person already appears to know or expect your answer.

Here's another great example. The losing football team of a World Cup final was once interviewed immediately after the match and the interviewer asked them, "Are you disappointed?" One of the team members wittily replied, "No, not at all. This is exactly what we hoped for—to get to the finals of the World Cup, and then lose." As you can see, the wit and hilarity of such a response derives from the fact that a resounding "yes" was expected, and yet the total opposite landed on the interviewer's ears.

These are questions that generally have an obvious answer, but the reason behind asking it is to receive an elaboration on the expected answer. This is why saying the opposite of what's expected is so effective. By giving the opposite answer, you completely throw off the other person. After a few moments, you can then give the real answer and say more about it.

Takeaways

- One of the main things that prevents us from being humorous and funny is that we take everything too literally, and we use boring language in doing so. This is a difference in mindset, similar to the play versus conversing/discussion dichotomy we had earlier. We miss easy opportunities when we can realize that some vocabulary choices are better than others, and that we have multiple chances a day to use them. So the first step in being funnier is to use language that is both specific and paints vivid images in people's minds.

- One comedy technique that relies on mental imagery is the comic triple. Here, you basically describe something using three adjectives, two positive, and one highly negative, in that order. Alternatively, X, Y, and opposite of X and Y. We generally expect a third related adjective after two consecutive ones, but an unrelated descriptor completely throws our audience off. The comic triple works because of the misdirection and surprise.

- The final technique is all about dissecting misdirection and how it can lead to big laughs. First, we start with sarcasm and irony. Sarcasm is when you say something you don't mean in an attempt to make fun or ridicule something. Irony, on the other hand, refers to situations where something happens that is the opposite of what you'd expect. This is more observational humor on your part, because you would be pointing out a contrast rather than creating one. Irony has a surprising amount of versatility because of the many places it can be applied. You can be on the lookout for ironic contrast between words and body language and tone, ironic hyperbole, and even use an ironic simile for yourself (lightweight as a brick).

Chapter 5. Captivating Stories

Captivating is a pretty strong word, and as such, it's probably something that we want to strive for in our interactions.

When we think of a captivating person, what kind of mental image comes to mind? If you were to choose a picture for a "captivating person" in a dictionary, what would the person be? What is this person expressing, how are they acting, and what are you watching them do?

More often than not, this person is going to

look like they are on a stage or pulpit gesticulating grandly and expressively, with an emotion-filled face. And I would also bet that this person is in the middle of weaving an engrossing tale that captivates his or her audience. Indeed, if you think about it, it seems that only with storytelling can we mesmerize and charm others into hanging on to our every word.

Okay, that's up for debate, but determining whether or not that is true is not the aim of this chapter. No one can deny that storytelling is an important element of memorable conversations and discussions that you want to have. The question is always how to capture this elusive skill and make it your own. Therefore, in this chapter, I want to present a few perspectives on how you can use storytelling in your everyday conversations and even small talk.

It's helpful to first take the mystique away from the whole concept of storytelling. What is storytelling? It's just telling someone about something that happened.

That's all. Of course, there are better and worse ways to do this, but at the core, storytelling is just talking about the past in a way that makes people pay attention. The first part we have no problem with—we've all described our pasts, and we all have great experiences worthy of being told—but the second part is typically the challenge. With that in mind, let's see how we can get better at storytelling.

A Life of Stories

To get better at stories, we have to begin to recognize them in our daily lives. No, seriously. We don't think of our lives as being very interesting on a day-to-day basis, but we do quite a bit more than we realize. It's not that every day you are engaging in a massive protest that you can tell your kids about, or you were chased by a wiener dog down a dark alley whereupon a man dressed as a parrot saved you by tackling the dog. These stories are self-evident and don't need any organization or special way of telling them to make an impact.

We have to draw from our daily lives, and believe me, there is plenty to draw from. It's just a matter of seeing the mini-stories that are inherent in our everyday existence. What is the definition of a mini-story in this context?

"So what do you do?"
"I'm a marketing executive."

Well, not that. That's going to get a reply of "Oh, cool. I'm going to the bathroom now, goodbye." Let's try again.

"So what do you do?"
"I'm a marketing executive. I deal mostly with clients. Just last week we had a crazy client that threatened to send his bodyguards to our office! I definitely wish I dealt more with the creative side."

There we go. This will probably garner a stronger response than wanting to escape to the bathroom, such as "Oh my God! Did he actually send them? TELL ME MORE."

That's a mini-story. It's answering questions (or spontaneously sharing) briefly using the elements of a story—an action that occurs to a subject with some sort of conclusion. As you can see above, a brief mini-story will create exponentially more conversation and interest than any answer to the question, "What do you do?" All you needed was three sentences. Try reading it out loud—it takes less than ten seconds, and you've jam-packed it with enough information to be interesting to anyone.

What's great about mini-stories is you can also create these before a conversation, so you can have compelling anecdotes at hand in response to very common and widespread questions. The main benefit to creating mini-stories ahead of time is to be able to avoid one-word answers that you may be accustomed to using. This can give a sense of confidence going in, because you've prepared for what will come.

When you break down the context surrounding a mini-story, they become much simpler. Shoot for three sentences that can answer some of the most common conversation topics that will arise.

1. Your occupation (if you have a job that is unusual or nebulous, make sure you have a layman's description of your job that people can relate to)
2. Your week
3. Your upcoming weekend
4. Your hometown
5. Your hobbies and so on.

When you are using a mini-story to answer a question, make sure to first acknowledge the question that was asked. But then, realizing that you have something far more interesting to say, you can jump into the mini-story, which should be able to stand by itself.

"How was your weekend?"
"It was fine. I watched four *Star Wars* movies."
"Okay, I'm going to go talk to someone else now."

Let's try again.

"How was your weekend?"
"It was fine, but did I tell you about what happened last Friday? A dog wearing a tuxedo walked into my office and he peed on everything."
"Wait. Tell me more."

Using mini-stories allows you to avoid the tired back of forth of "Good, how about you" you'll find in everyday small talk. That's the first step to being captivating.

It might help to reframe mini-stories this way: when people make small talk with you and ask any of the classic small-talk questions, they aren't truly interested in the answers to those questions. They want to hear something interesting, so give it to them.

This is an important point to repeat: when we ask how someone's weekend was, or what people's travel plans are, we usually aren't that interested in the literal answer. We've already talked about how you should disclose and divulge more about yourself in an effort to find more similarities, and now you can see another benefit of offering more.

Not only that, mini-stories are an inside view to the way you think and feel. They give clues to your mindset, personality, and emotional leanings. Learning about those aspects is the first step in allowing anyone to relate and feel connected to you, so it's imperative that you learn how to take any question and expand it to your advantage. It will also encourage them to reciprocate.

Mini-stories also underscore the importance of providing more details, as mentioned in an earlier chapter, and avoiding one-word answers. Details offer a three-dimensional description of you and your life. That automatically makes people more interested and invested because they are already painting a mental picture in their minds and visualizing everything.

Details also give people more to connect to, think about, and attach themselves to. With more details, there is a substantially higher likelihood that people will find something funny, interesting, in common, poignant, curious, and worthy of comment in what you have to say.

Detail and specificity put people into a particular place and time. This allows them to imagine exactly what's happening and start caring about it. Think about why it's so easy to get sucked into a movie. We experience enormous sensory stimulation and almost can't escape all of the visual and auditory detail, which is designed to make us invested. Detailed stories and conversations are inviting others to share a mental movie with you.

Beyond giving flavor to your conversation and storytelling, and giving the other person something to ask about, details are important because they elicit emotional engagement. Details remind people of their own lives and memories and make them feel more drawn to whatever is presenting them. Details can compel others to laugh, feel mad, feel sad, or feel surprise. They can control moods and emotions.

If you include details about specific songs that played during your high school dances, it's likely that someone will have memories attached to those songs and become more emotionally interested in your story. Share details about all the figurative nooks and crannies, because that's what makes you interesting on an emotional level.

The 1:1:1 Method

On the theme of simplifying storytelling, we've been talking about how we can use a mini-story in many ways. You may be wondering what the difference is between a *mini* story and a *full-fledged* story.

For our purposes, not much. It seems that many people like to complicate storytelling as if they were composing an impromptu Greek tragedy. Does there have to be an introduction, middle, struggle, then resolution? Does there need to be a hero, a conflict, and an emotional journey? Not necessarily. Those are specific ways of storytelling if you are Francis Ford Coppola (director of the *Godfather* series) or a standup comedian used to keeping crowds engaged.

But certainly these aren't the easiest or most practical ways to think about storytelling.

My method of storytelling in conversation is to prioritize the discussion afterward. This means that the story itself doesn't need to be that in-depth or long. It can and should contain specific details that people can relate to and latch on to, but it doesn't need to have parts or stages. A full story can be *mini* by nature. That's why it's called the *1:1:1 method.*

This method stands for a story that (1) has one action, (2) can be summed up in one sentence, and (3) evokes one primary emotion in the listener. You can see why they're short and snappy. They also tend to ensure that you know your point before starting and have a very low chance of verbally wandering for minutes and alienating your listeners. This is the lowest input to the highest output ratio you can have for a story.

For a story to consist of *one action* means only one thing is happening. The story is about one occurrence, one event. It should be direct and straightforward. Anything else just confuses the point and makes you liable to ramble. Details are important to share, but probably not at the outset because the story's impact will be lost or blunted.

A story should be able to be *summed up* in one sentence because, otherwise, you are trying to convey too much. It keeps you focused and straight to the point. This step actually takes practice, because you are forced to think about which aspects of the story matter and which don't add anything to your action. It's a skill to be able to distill your thoughts into one sentence and still be thorough—often, you won't realize what you want to say unless you can do this.

Finally, a story should focus on one primary emotion to be evoked in the listener. And you should be able to name it! Keep in mind that evoking an emotion ensures that your story actually has a point, and it will color what details you carefully choose to emphasize that emotion. For our purposes here, there really aren't that many emotions you might want to draw out in others from a story. You might have humor, shock, awe, envy, happiness, anger, or annoyance. Those are the majority of reasons we relate our experiences to others.

Keep in mind that this is just my method for conveying my experiences to others. My logic is that whether people hear two sentences about a dog attack or they hear ten sentences doesn't change the impact of the story. Telling a story about your friend going to jail—well, he's still in jail at the end of two or ten sentences. Likewise, if you tell a story about how you adopted a dog, the dog will still be lounging on your bed if you take ten seconds or two minutes to tell the story.

After you provide the premise, the conversation can move forward as a dialogue, your conversation partner can participate more fully, and we can then focus on the listener's impact and reaction. Then you can let the inevitable questions flow, and you can slowly divulge the details after the context is set, and the initial impact is felt. So what does this so-called story sound like?

"I was attacked by a dog and I was so frightened I nearly wet my pants." It's one sentence, there is one action, and the bit about wetting the pants is to emphasize the fact that the emotion you want to convey is fear and shock.

You could include more detail about the dog and the circumstances, but chances are people are going to ask about that immediately, so let them guide what they want to hear about your story. It doesn't hurt to directly name the emotion that you were experiencing. Invite them to participate! Very few people want to sit and listen to a monologue, most of which is told poorly and in a scattered manner. Therefore, keep the essentials but cut your story short, and let the conversation continue as a shared experience rather than you monopolizing the airspace. Here are another couple of easy examples:

"Last week, I had a job interview that went so poorly I had the interviewer laugh at me while I was leaving the office, it was so embarrassing." One action, one emotion, in one sentence.

"When I first met Joshua, I spilled a bowl of baked beans all over his white pants and I think the entire room was watching while this happened."

The 1:1:1 method can be summed up as starting a story as close to the end as possible. Most stories end before they get to the end, in terms of impact on the listener, their attention span, and the energy that you have to tell it. In other words, many stories tend to drone on because people try to adhere to complex rules or because they simply lose the plot and are trying to find it again through talking. Above all else, a long preamble is not necessary. What's important is that people pay attention, care, and will react in some (preferably) emotional manner.

The Story Spine

Think of the story spine as an upgraded and expanded version of the 1:1:1 method. It gives you the beats of a great story in a simple formula.

This technique can be credited to Kevin Adams, *author and the artistic director of Synergy Theater. He teaches how the "story spine" can be used to outline a great story. This method is perfect for novelists and film makers, but you can also use it whenever you want to entertain friends with a tale that will have them riveted. Likewise, it can tell you why certain stories completely fall flat, since it shows you what crucial elements may be missing. It can be done quickly and, with practice, may start feeling automatic.*

The story spine has eight elements; here's how they go:

Once upon a time...

The start of the story. Here, you must set the context and lay out the world you're talking about and the characters you'll be focusing on. You establish their routine, normal reality. If you skip this part your story may seem inconsequential, or people won't be able to make sense of the events that follow and why they matter.

Every day...

More establishing of the normal and routine. Often, a character is growing bored, sad or curious, and this drives the next stages of the story. This step builds tension, and is the place you give your characters a personality and a motive for what happens next.

But one day...

And here comes the big event that changes everything! One day, something different happens that completely turns your character's world around. A stranger comes to town or a mysterious clue shows up.

Because of that...

There are consequences. The main character acts in response, and this sets into motion the main body of the story, the "what happened" part. Many poor storytellers will simply leap in and begin here, failing to build tension or set any context, and then discover that their audience isn't as invested in the outcome. Like good conversation skills, good storytelling skills require pacing and *gradual* building of tension.

Because of that...

Things get more interesting or frightening, the stakes are raised, the plot thickens, other characters enter and a whole world of complications/comedy/drama opens up as the story plays out.

Because of that...

Good stories appeal to our love for the number three in our narratives. That's why we have Goldilocks and the three bears, and why the hero typically faces three challenges before finally making it. Take the time to really explore the three dilemmas the character faces, and you make the resolution that much sweeter.

Until finally...

Does the guy get the girl? Was the world saved or did the detective find out who did it? Here's where you reveal all. The conflict is resolved, and the story is wrapped up.

And ever since then...

You close the story as you began it—with some context. You outline here what the new normal is, given the character's success or failure at the previous step. You could consider a moral of the story here, or a little joke or punchline. In conversation, this tells people you're done with your story and signals them to respond.

What's important to remember about a story spine is that it's just that—a spine.

You still need to add considerable flesh to the outline to make it compelling. The story spine merely makes sure you're hitting the right notes in the right order, and gives you a satisfying structure to follow. Not every story will follow it exactly (it's only a rough outline, after all) but if yours do, there's a good chance they'll be better received than narratives that are a bit more experimental.

As an example, consider the popular theme song for the '80s TV show *The Fresh Prince of Bel-Air*. This shows that even in a quick story, it's important to have the essential building blocks. The song starts:

In west Philadelphia born and raised
On the playground is where I spent most of
my days
Chillin' out maxin' relaxin' all cool
And all shootin' some b-ball outside of the
school

This covers "once upon a time" and "every day." Context established.

When a couple of guys who were up to no

good
Started makin' trouble in my neighborhood
I got in one little fight and my mom scared
And said you're movin' with your auntie and
uncle in Bel-Air

Here's the "but one day" part that changes
everything.

I begged and pleaded with her day after day
But she packed my suitcase and sent me on
my way... etc.

The middle portion of the song covers him
begging with his mom not to go, getting on a
plane to Bel-Air and then taking a cab, while
slowly grasping the whole new world he's
just walked into. This is the middle of the
story, the three "and because of that"
portions. The final verse goes:

I pulled up to the house about 7 or 8
And I yelled to the cabbie yo homes smell ya
later
Looked at my kingdom I was finally there
To sit on my throne as the prince of Bel-Air

"And finally" and "since then" are rolled into one here, and the new normal is established, with the main character happily set up in his new life. Granted, there isn't too much conflict or tension here, but the structure is sound.

Consider someone using the story spine in a more everyday context: a dispute at work. Someone is trying to explain what's happened clearly to an external mediator. Their story sounds like this:

"Melissa and Jake both work in the IT department, they run things together with Barbara, who's now on maternity leave. Melissa's been with the company for more than ten years, and Jake is new, so Melissa has been informally training him to cover Barbara's work for the next six months, possibly longer term (there are rumors Jake will get Barbara's job if she leaves). They've been working on a big project together for the last month.

"Unknown to us, Melissa and Jake had a brief relationship months back that ended badly.

"Because of that there's been some tension in the office. There was a crucial mistake on the big project and Melissa was held accountable. But she's since revealed to us that it was in fact Jake's fault, and she had covered for him while they were still in a relationship. Because of this, Jake is claiming that Melissa is only blaming him now because they are no longer in a relationship, which he believes is unfair.

"Eventually, Barbara contacted the office to let them know she wasn't returning, a condition Mark assumed would solidify his role in the office. But now there's a big conflict as both Melissa and Jake can barely stand to work together."

In this story, the mediator is hearing the final stages, but the "and ever since" part is yet to be decided. Can you see the steps, and how leaving any of them out or mixing them up might have made for a more confusing story?

Consider the box office hit *Avatar*, and how it follows the story spine:

Once upon a time there was a paraplegic Marine called Jake Sully with a traumatic past, who was just getting by in life. Every day he mourned the tragic death of his brilliant and talented brother.

But one day, he gets the opportunity to join a mission to distant moon Pandora. Because of that, he is promised surgery that will allow him to walk again in exchange for gathering info on the species that lives on the planet, the Na'Vi.

Because of that, he spends more time with them, eventually developing a real love for their world as well as for the beautiful Neytiri. Because of that love, he is unable to take part in the (soon-to-be-discovered) exploitative nature of the expedition, until finally, a full-blown war breaks out between humans and the Na'Vi. Finally, the battle is won, and Pandora is saved. And ever since then, Jake has lived in peace on Pandora.

Naturally, there are many details and

elements missing here, but the spine is intact and is partly responsible for a story that is engaging and plays out in a way the audience expects. The story spine applies to any kind of story or narrative, written, spoken or cinematic, big or small. The fundamentals, once in place, can be reworked in literally endless ways.

Inside Stories

In any conversation, there is a high point. There might be multiple memorable points, but by definition, one part is the best and highest.

This can take many different forms. You can share a big laugh. You can both get emotional and cry. You share a strong perspective on an issue that no one else does. You witness something either horrifying or hilarious together. You both struggle not to laugh when you observe something. You finish each other's sentences. Most of the time, if you do it correctly, your stories become high points because of the emotional impact and pure intrigue you can use them to create. This makes it easy because you are planting the seed of connection for you to harvest later.

Coincidentally, calling back to this high point later is what a deconstructed *inside joke* looks like. Therefore, to easily create an inside joke, all you have to do is refer to the high point later in the conversation. Take note of it and put it in your pocket for use in the near future. Don't let it go sour like month-old milk that you're afraid to throw away because of the smell. Assuming that you told a good story or elicited a good story earlier in the conversation, all you need to do is refer to it in the context of your current topic.

For example, you told a story about your favorite kind of dog earlier in the conversation. There was a high point about comparing yourself to a wiener dog because your shape makes it unavoidable.

Now your current topic of conversation is fashion, personal style and different types of jackets. How do you call back to the wiener dog high point by referring to it in the context of jackets? *"Yeah, unfortunately, I can't wear that type of jacket because I'm mostly similar to the wiener dog, remember?"*

Bring up the first topic, hopefully the topic of your story, and then use it in the current subject. You are repeating the old topic in a new context, and this tends to be better received, even if it wasn't funny the first time. And the best part is that you can keep doing this with the same thing to create an even stronger unique bond (inside joke!).

Listen for something funny or notable that you would classify as a conversational high point. Keep it in your pocket. Wait like a cheetah in the tall grass of the savannah to see a different context or topic you can repeat it in. And then unleash it.

Here's another example.

Prior conversational high point: a story about hating parking lots.

Current topic of conversation: the weather.

Callback: *Yeah, the rain will definitely be welcome when we can't find parking spots within ten blocks of our apartment.*

And here's one more:

Prior conversational high point: a story about loving donuts.

Current topic of conversation: hating work.

Callback: Well what if your office provided free donuts? How many would you need to change your opinion of work?

In the same way an orchestra conductor can hit the same high musical motif through different arrangements and songs, you can keep referring to this conversation high point. Voila, you've just created an inside joke from thin air.

Ask for Stories

Most of the focus with stories is usually on

telling them—but what about soliciting them from others and allowing them to feel as good as you do when a story lands well? What about stepping aside and giving other people the spotlight (an underrated skill in conversation and life in general)? Well, it's just a matter of how you ask for other's stories. There are ways to make people gab for hours, and approaches where people will feel compelled to give a terse one-word answer.

For instance, when you watch sports, one of the most illogical parts is the post-game or post-match interview. These athletes are still caught in the throes of adrenaline, out of breath, and occasionally drip sweat onto the reporters. It's not a situation conducive to good stories, or even answers.

Yet when you are watching a broadcaster interview an athlete, does anything odd strike you about the questions they ask? The interviewers are put into an impossible situation and usually walk away with decent soundbites—at the very least, not audio disasters. Their duty is to elicit a coherent answer from someone who is mentally incoherent at the moment. How do they do that?

They'll ask questions like "So tell me about that moment in the second quarter. What did you feel about it and how did the coach turn it around then?" as opposed to "How'd you guys win?" or "How did you turn this match around, come back, and pull out all the stops to grab the victory at the very end?" as opposed to "How was the comeback?"

The key? They ask for a story rather than an answer. They phrase their inquiry in a way that can only be answered with a story, in fact.

Reporters provide the athletes with detail, context, and boundaries to set them up to talk as much as possible instead of providing a breathless one-word answer. It's almost as if they provide the athletes with an outline of what they want to hear and how they can proceed. They make it easy for them to tell a story and simply engage. It's like if someone asks you a question but, in the question, tells you exactly what they want to hear as hints.

Sometimes we think we are doing the heavy lifting in a conversation and the other party isn't giving us much to work with. But that's an excuse that obscures the fact we aren't making it easy for them. They might not be giving you much, but you also might be asking them the wrong questions, which is leading them to provide terrible responses. In fact, if you think you are shouldering the burden, you are definitely asking the wrong questions.

Conversation can be much more pleasant for everyone involved if you provide fertile ground for people to work in. Don't set the other person up to fail and be a poor conversationalist; that will only make you invest and care less and cause the conversation to die out.

When people ask me low-effort, vague questions, I know they probably aren't interested in the answer. They're just filling the time and silence. To create win-win conversations and better circumstances for all, ask for stories the way the sports broadcasters do. Ask questions in a way that makes people want to share.

Stories are personal, emotional, and compelling. There is a thought process and narrative that necessarily exists. They are what show your personality and are how you can learn about someone. They reveal people's emotions and how they think. Last but not least, they show what you care about.

Compare this with simply asking for closed-ended answers. These answers are often too boring and routine for people to care. They will still respond to your questions but in a very literal way, and the level of engagement won't be there. Peppering people with shallow questions puts them in a position to fail conversationally.

It's the difference between asking "What was the best part of your day so far? Tell me how you got that parking space so close!"

instead of just "How are you?"

When you ask somebody the second question, you're looking for a quick, uninvolved answer. You're being lazy and either don't care about their answer or want them to carry the conversational burden. When you ask somebody one of the first two questions, you're inviting them to tell a specific story about their day. You are encouraging them to narrate the series of events that made their day great or not. And your query can't really be covered with a one-word answer.

Another example is "What is the most exciting part of your job? How does it feel to make a difference like that?" instead of simply asking them the generic "What do you do?" When you only ask somebody what they do for a living, you know exactly how the rest of the conversation will go: "Oh, I do X. What about you?"

A final example is "How did you feel about your weekend? What was the best part? It was so nice outside," instead of just "How was your weekend?"

Prompting others for stories instead of simple answers gives them a chance to speak in such a way that they feel emotionally invested. This increases the sense of meaning they derive from the conversation. It also makes them feel you are genuinely interested in hearing their answer because your question doesn't sound generic.

Consider the following guidelines when asking a question:

1. Ask for a story
2. Be broad but with specific directions or prompts
3. Ask about feelings and emotions
4. Give the other person a direction to expand their answer into, and give them multiple prompts, hints, and possibilities
5. If all else fails, directly ask "Tell me the story about..."

Imagine that you want the other person to inform your curiosity. Other examples include the following:

1. "Tell me about the time you..." versus "How was that?"
2. "Did you like that..." versus "How was it?"
3. "You look focused. What happened in your morning..." versus "How are you?"

Let's think about what happens when you elicit (and provide) personal stories instead of the old, tired automatic replies.

You say hello to your coworker on Monday morning and you ask how his weekend was. At this point, you have cataloged what you will say in case he asks you the same. Remember, the person probably doesn't care about the actual answer ("good" or "okay"), but they *would* like to hear something interesting. But you never get the chance, because you ask him "How was your weekend? Tell me about the most interesting part—I know you didn't just watch a movie at home!"

He opens up and begins to tell you about his

Saturday night when he separately and involuntarily visited a strip joint, a funeral, and a child's birthday party. That's a conversation that can take off and get interesting, and you've successfully bypassed the unnecessary and boring small talk that plagues so many of us.

Most people love talking about themselves. Use this fact to your advantage. Once someone takes your cue and starts sharing a story, make sure you are aware of how you're responding to that person through your facial expressions, gestures, body language, and other nonverbal signals. Since there is always at least one exciting thing in any story, focus on that high point and don't be afraid to show that you're engaged.

One quick tip to show that you're involved and even willing to add to the conversation is something I call *pinning the tail on the donkey*. There is probably a better name for it, but it will suffice for the time being. The donkey is the story from someone else, while the tail is your addition to it. It allows you to feel like you're contributing, it makes other people know you're listening, and it turns into something you've created together. In essence, you are taking the impact that someone wants to convey, and you are amplifying it. You are assisting them in their own storytelling—they want to extract a specific reaction from you, and you are going above and beyond with the *tail*.

People will actually love you for it because, when you do this, your mindset becomes focused on assisting people's stories and letting them have the floor. Here's an example:

Bob's story: "I went to the bank and tripped and spilled all my cash, making it rain inadvertently."

Tail: **"Did you think you were Scrooge McDuck for a second?"**

When you make a tail, try to hone in on the primary emotion the story was conveying, then add a comment that amplifies it. The story was about how Bob felt rich, and Scrooge McDuck is a duck who swims in pools of gold doubloons, so it adds to the story and doesn't steal Bob's thunder.

Sabrina's story: "After I ate lunch, I ran into the president of my company and he said he remembered me because of the great ideas I had at the last meeting!"

Tail: "Just like you were winning a beauty pageant!"

This story was about how Sabrina felt flattered and hopeful, and so the concept of a beauty pageant amplifies these emotions. Get into the habit of assisting other people's stories. It's easy, witty, and extremely appealing because you are helping them out.

Takeaways:

- Captivating people usually refers to telling a story that leaves them listening like children (in a good way). Storytelling is a big topic that is often made overly complex, but there are many ways of creating this feeling in small, everyday ways. To captivate others is no easy feat, but the material and ability lies within all of us. We just have to know where it is and how to access it.

- An easy way to imagine everyday storytelling is that your life is a series of stories—mini-stories, to be exact. Instead of giving one-word answers, get into the habit of framing your answers as a story with a point. It creates more engagement, lets you show your personality, and allows for smoother conversation. The bonus here is that you can prepare these before a conversation.
- The 1:1:1 method of storytelling is to simplify it as much as possible. The impact of a story won't necessarily be stronger if it is ten sentences versus two sentences. Therefore, the 1:1:1: method focuses on the discussion and reaction that occurs after a story. A story can be composed solely of (1) one action, (2) one emotion to be evoked, and (3) a one-sentence summary. Don't get lost

rambling, and also make sure your listener feels that they are fully participating in the conversation.

- The story spine is more or less the formula for every movie that exists. It's a simple framework that you can use in your everyday stories and conversations, because it teaches you what emotional beats exist in a story. There is the status quo, the event that kicks things off, the set of consequences for changing the status quo, the climax or resolution, and then what happens after the fact.

- Stories can also be the basis for an inside joke. When you think about it, an inside joke is something that comes up multiple times with the same person and evokes a positive emotion. It's the same topic brought up in a different context. Thus, you just need to call back to a story through a conversation and there's a good chance it will stick as a "Remember when we talked about..." moment. The more you use it, the more a unique bond is created between only the two of you.

- Improving your storytelling ability is important, but what about eliciting stories from others? You can phrase your questions carefully to ask for stories rather than answers from people, which is a simple way to make conversation easier and more enjoyable for everyone involved. There are ways to make people open up to you and want to keep gabbing. Remember the lesson we learned with the 1:1:1 method in pinpointing the emotions that people are trying to evoke. To amplify this, you can *pin the tail on the donkey* and strategically add on to people's stories.

Summary Guide

Chapter 1. Flow Like a River

- You know those people who always have something clever or witty to say? Ever wonder how they cultivated this seemingly magical quality? If you have, know that being witty is much easier than you might think, and you don't have to be born with the gift of gab. By following certain tricks and techniques, you can develop the same persona yourself. The first element to tackle is conversational flow and keeping a back and forth going.
- The first trick in the book is to never speak in absolutes. Eliminate questions and statements involving words like favorite, absolute, only, worst, etc., from your vocabulary. If you ask someone "what's your absolute favorite movie?", you are actually asking a pressurized question that introduces pause and

destroys flow. Instead, always generalize your questions by putting boundaries and constraints on them. This doesn't require as much thought from your conversational partner, allowing them to simply answer a question with a range of responses instead of being caught looking for the one "right" answer.

- Reactions are important. People say and do things for a reason, and it's usually to get a reaction. This step is deceptively simple yet difficult. Pay attention to other people and ask yourself what emotion they want to evoke. Then give it to them. Don't take too long to reply, but being too quick isn't advisable either. This is all to make others feel that you are present and engaged.

- If your mind goes blank, use a technique called free association to generate a response. These are words that immediately come to mind upon hearing something. For example, if someone talks about cats, practice free association with the provided exercises, and you'll be able to come up with answers more quickly and easily. Conversation as a whole is just a series of interrelated responses and stories, so free association is practicing conversation flow.

- Regardless of who you're talking to, you're likely to be asked the same set of generic questions. These include what do you do, how was your day, and others like these. You'll want to have two separate answers prepared for such questions, one of which is interesting and unique (the layman explanation), while the other is more informative (the expert explanation). Being too esoteric upon first meeting someone isn't always helpful, and can confuse and render others speechless.

- Finally, learn to give good compliments. This is also deceptively easy. Compliment things that people have control over, or made a choice about. Don't choose genetic qualities like height or eye color; instead choose things that people actively put effort into. People feel comfortable and flattered, and then start to open up.

Chapter 2. Conversation Is Play

- All of conversation is an opportunity for playful interaction. It just takes a shift in mindset to see that, and the world will open up.
- Breaking the fourth wall is a simple, yet effective move to make any conversation more interesting. Often used in movies, this technique essentially involves commenting about the conversation you're having in some positive way. This is generally something that both parties are thinking but has gone unacknowledged. If you're having a particularly funny conversation with someone, you might jokingly remark, "Things have really escalated, haven't they?" This is a great way to connect as it shows that you're aware of your conversations on a deeper level.
- Next, we have the 'Us Against the World' technique. This one entails forming an in-group with the person you're talking to based on some common experience or emotion that

both of you share. If, say, you're both at a club where the music is too loud, you can comment something like "These people seem to be getting along fine, but I'm sure we're both going to lose our hearing soon!" This forms a shared experience and inside joke that can be used in future interactions as well.

- If a conversation seems to be dying out or droning along, you might want to have some fallback stories to reinvigorate your interaction. These are extremely short incidents that you can narrate to get the other person's opinion or ask how they'd react in the same situation. The emphasis here is on the discussion and opinion. For example, you can tell them about how a girl broke with stereotypes and proposed to her boyfriend, following it up with a question on what they'd do in a similar situation. This can spark a surprising conversation.
- We also have instant role playing as a technique that you can fall back on.

This is perhaps one of the easiest tricks mentioned so far. The trick generally involves both of you taking up some generic roles and playing them out for comedic relief. There are four steps to consider here. First, compliment the other person on some quality that they have, like being a great navigator. Then, assign them a role based on this quality, say being like Magellan. This is the role they'll play, that of a renowned navigator. Simply follow this up with interesting questions about navigation ("Which continent did you enjoy discovering most?") and pull them into the role play.

Chapter 3. A Touch of Witty Banter

- This chapter will teach you how to be a witty comeback machine. If you're the kind of person who thinks of smart replies twenty minutes after a conversation ends, the techniques laid out here will help you come up with them much quicker. It's a matter of thinking non-literally, non-conventionally, and non-linearly, and realizing that a conversation is an opportunity for play rather than information dissemination.

- If someone is teasing you, there are two methods you can use which will help you come up with a witty comeback. You can either take the thing they're teasing you about and exaggerate it to the point of absurdity, or point out a funny, but positive side effect of that thing you're being teased about.

- While delivering comebacks, it's important to use the right tone and act like you can take a joke. Nobody likes a bad sport, and you'll want to indicate that you're joking through your demeanor and expressions. Smile wryly after saying your comeback, and use a tone that conveys indifference rather than annoyance.

- Our next few tricks rely on the art of misconstruing. The banter chain is the first of these. Banter chains are a series of exchanges that rely on you having misconstrued an ordinary remark as the other person plays along. You put forth a purposeful misinterpretation, and if they bite on it, you have now entered what you can call a banter chain, and can continue to ramp it up.

- Another technique relying on misconstruing is the exaggerated conclusion. Here, you basically take a statement and exaggerate it exponentially to step out of the ordinary and into something that can resemble play. Our last misconstruing trick is the playful tease, where you give your conversation partner a bit of good-natured ribbing that leaves you both laughing.

Chapter 4. Funny on Command

- One of the main things that prevents us from being humorous and funny is that we take everything too literally, and we use boring language in doing so. This is a difference in mindset, similar to the play versus conversing/discussion dichotomy we had earlier. We miss easy opportunities when we can realize that some vocabulary choices are better than others, and that we have multiple chances a day to use them. So the first step in being funnier is to use language that is both specific and paints vivid images in people's minds.

- One comedy technique that relies on mental imagery is the comic triple. Here, you basically describe something using three adjectives, two positive, and one highly negative, in that order. Alternatively, X, Y, and opposite of X and Y. We generally expect a third related adjective after two consecutive ones, but an unrelated descriptor completely throws our audience off. The comic triple works because of the misdirection and surprise.
- The final technique is all about dissecting misdirection and how it can lead to big laughs. First, we start with sarcasm and irony. Sarcasm is

when you say something you don't mean in an attempt to make fun or ridicule something. Irony, on the other hand, refers to situations where something happens that is the opposite of what you'd expect. This is more observational humor on your part, because you would be pointing out a contrast rather than creating one. Irony has a surprising amount of versatility because of the many places it can be applied. You can be on the lookout for ironic contrast between words and body language and tone, ironic hyperbole, and even use an ironic simile for yourself (lightweight as a brick).

Chapter 5. Captivating Stories

- Captivating people usually refers to telling a story that leaves them listening like children (in a good way). Storytelling is a big topic that is often made overly complex, but there are many ways of creating this feeling in small, everyday ways. To captivate others is no easy feat, but the material and ability lies within all of us. We just have to know where it is and how to access it.

- An easy way to imagine everyday storytelling is that your life is a series of stories—mini-stories, to be exact. Instead of giving one-word answers, get into the habit of framing your answers as a story with a point. It creates more engagement, lets you show your personality, and allows for smoother conversation. The bonus here is that you can prepare these before a conversation.

- The 1:1:1 method of storytelling is to simplify it as much as possible. The impact of a story won't necessarily be stronger if it is ten sentences versus two sentences. Therefore, the 1:1:1: method focuses on the discussion and reaction that occurs after a story. A story can be composed solely of (1) one action, (2) one emotion to be evoked, and (3) a one-sentence summary. Don't get lost rambling, and also make sure your listener feels that they are fully participating in the conversation.

- The story spine is more or less the formula for every movie that exists. It's a simple framework that you can use in your everyday stories and conversations, because it teaches you what emotional beats exist in a story. There is the status quo, the event that kicks things off, the set of consequences for changing the status quo, the climax or resolution, and then what happens after the fact.

- Stories can also be the basis for an inside joke. When you think about it, an inside joke is something that comes up multiple times with the same person and evokes a positive emotion. It's the same topic brought up in a different context.

Thus, you just need to call back to a story through a conversation and there's a good chance it will stick as a "Remember when we talked about..." moment. The more you use it, the more a unique bond is created between only the two of you.

- Improving your storytelling ability is important, but what about eliciting stories from others? You can phrase your questions carefully to ask for stories rather than answers from people, which is a simple way to make conversation easier and more enjoyable for everyone involved. There are ways to make people open up to you and want to keep gabbing. Remember the lesson we learned with the 1:1:1 method in pinpointing the emotions that people are trying to evoke. To amplify this, you can *pin the tail on the donkey* and strategically add on to people's stories.